YOU CAN WRITE A STEP-BY-STEP HOUSE OF WORSHIP EMERGENCY SAFETY AND SECURITY PLAN

LAUREN HOLLEY-ALLEN, MA, PSA

ISBN 978-1-0980-8275-8 (paperback)
ISBN 978-1-0980-8276-5 (hardcover)
ISBN 978-1-0980-8277-2 (digital)

Christian Faith Publishing, Inc.
832 Park Avenue
Meadville, PA 16335
www.christianfaithpublishing.com

Printed in the United States of America

To Amber D. Taylor-Hamid,
my youngest daughter, who encouraged me to continue writing this
book in December 2019, after I developed floaters in my right eye.

CONTENTS

ACKNOWLEDGMENTS

I want to express my gratitude to my favorite authors whose books I read to acquaint and encourage my cultivating the needed skills and nuances of writing.

Robert Caro's 2019 book titled *Working*, which I read on a cruise ship. Among other skills, he taught me to turn every page and never skimp on my reader audiences.

Jean Marie Stein's book titled *Writing Successful Self Help & How to Books* taught me everything I needed to know when I had no one to ask.

Pastor Bobby Cox Jr. said he was proud to be my pastor which gives me the courage to continue God's book for his people.

Thank you is certainly due to the myriad of creative online federal agency resources, available in the public domain.

I would also like to thank my colleagues at Maryland Emergency Management Agency, Clifton T. Perkins Forensic Hospital, and especially Christine Jefferies who mentored me at Rosewood State Hospital in 1985, when I first began working as a master's-level psychologist with Special Needs Adolescents.

A special thanks is due to Kevin Anderson & Associates: Mark Weinstein, Editorial Director, SVP, and the editorial team of Kevin Zambrano, Project Manager.

Editor Brunella Costagliola, I will always hold you close to my heart for being a good listener when I felt insecure.

Thanks are also due to Melissa Wheeling, publication specialist and, the Christian Faith Publishing team.

INTRODUCTION

Why Do We Need Emergency Management Planning?

Do you know what to do in case of an emergency? If a hate crime occurs in your house of worship or a tornado hits it or a pandemic suddenly threatens your congregation, would you know what to do? An emergency management plan is needed to mitigate either known or perceived risks and the possibility of adverse results that could take place. The danger of any potential emergency event—including a fire or a pandemic—could endanger a house of worship's ability to function and serve the community. The plan should focus on measures that address the degree of probability—as high, medium, low, or as most likely, likely or unlikely—categorized under each risk to assess the severity of an incident and implement steps to eliminate the problem or curtail the effects of potential threats or hazards.

Emergency management planning includes determining potential emergency situations, a developing creative appropriate response to each with written scenario planning. Required resources should be preplanned as we recently learned during a worldwide pandemic. However, planning for other emergencies we have more experience and success in response planning for—such as fire safety or weather advisories—seems less catastrophic.

The clergy must address disasters on a regular basis, and they are now required to obtain additional emergency management information, training, and writing skills they may not have trained for or have any interest in. As a result, they are challenged to absorb information needed to manage and prepare their congregations.

Conducting a continuity of operation plan and a business impact analysis can help a house of worship understand what they are up against and mitigate potential risks posed by various events.

After the emergency has occurred and the congregants with clergy have responded to the emergency event, they are faced with additional challenges, which could potentially result in them not feeling ready to move into the recovery phase.

Houses of worship are typically a place that provides their members with comfort and inspiration. Most of the congregants who attend places of worship expect to find peace and solace. Unfortunately, disasters and emergencies can strike at any place or time. An emergency or disaster could have devastating long-lasting effects on houses of worship worldwide and impacts could include injury or loss of life, not to mention the negative emotional consequences on congregants, family members, and the nation. Other threats are the damage or loss of the facility, damage of equipment or furnishings, loss of personal property, loss of revenue, or loss of donations. In 2019, to mitigate the potential impacts on my house of worship and community, I outlined the first draft of our emergency plan. The purpose was to address potential disasters and emergencies that may impact our edifice, congregants, and leadership.

The problem I experienced in writing my first emergency plan was a lack of available information and how to best write, develop, or implement the plan. The literature I researched gave minimal guidance regarding what our house of worship needed to include within the plan about fire safety, evacuation, weather emergencies, OSHA regulations, firearm protocols, and other potential questions that might arise. In addition, after writing the plan, there was no concise information as to how it should be taught, trained, or implemented.

This book will serve as a guide for congregants and anyone who has little or minimal experience in the following: training, emergency management, security, psychology, public health, or mental health background. In this book, I intend to include all the necessary information so to guide readers' understanding of a technical subject in a nontechnical format. The lay community can write a plan following step-by-step guidelines.

Most available checklists direct us to follow conventional wisdom and protocols, thus suggesting we approach the subject like every other house of worship. The question is whether this conventional wisdom is best for your houses of worship. For a time, while writing the plan, I subscribed to the conventional wisdom of various checklist and did not consider there might be other creative approaches in writing a plan.

This book will guide you through the process of writing, developing, training, and implementing your house of worship's emergency safety and security plan that works for your edifice and congregants. The basic tasks necessary to succeed are at your fingertips. Various religious denominations will also benefit (i.e., churches, synagogues, mosques, temples, parishes, and most if not all, congregations).

The primary goal is to assist clergy and lay leaders with administration in their efforts to manage and prepare for most emergencies and implement common-sense planning. We are taking a different approach in guiding the reader through a process for both inexperienced and experienced writers.

The Training Process

The current political climate and increased safety and security issues are of international concern. The environment in soft targets (i.e., synagogues, temples, churches, mosques, movie theatres, schools, and shopping centers) has become increasingly toxic. These targets are the focus of emergency managers everywhere.

These guidelines are designed to address basic procedures for your beginning planning process. It will take time to write and eventually implement these steps, and how long it takes is up to you and your individual places of worship. If you are expecting quick overnight success, you are not reading the right book. *This is a process.*

Project Management in Nontechnical Language

Many people might not choose to spend the time going through this or any process that is not short-term with quick results. Short-term projects generally take a few hours to weeks to complete. Effective managers begin by assessing the need to determine the amount of time needed to achieve the desired outcomes. Long-term projects require additional or more documentation, research, manpower (assistance), and time to complete. This project is ongoing as you will evolve and experience the need to update the plan after each emergency event, training, or drill at least biannually or annually.

The Skills Needed and How It Is Done

The written safety and security plan developed for my congregation from beginning to end was a yearlong process. It was marked by gradual changes as I collaborated with teams of people in primary leadership and support roles. Overall, it required many months of rewrites before I was able to submit a final draft to leadership. The planning was a series of operations in which I was required to wait for input from other actors. Some were directly and others indirectly involved in the process. I waited to proceed while taking minuscule steps during the research and writing process. I worked with others with differing personalities, individual perspectives, and aptitudes—which tested my patience and humility. It is not enough to discuss the actual plan as simply textbook strategic plan development. It is important that you understand the time commitment and emotional cost involved, as well as what it takes to write and execute the plan, and the specific skills needed to put it into practice as a course of action. No one taught or told me. I had to learn this by reading manuals, publications, trial and error—including the school of hard knocks. Be encouraged, if you focus on the right process for your specific environment in the right way and with the right motives for beginning the task, you can and will design your emergency safety and security plan successfully.

The Role of Leadership (Clergy)

Clergy professionals are spiritual leaders in the Catholic, Sikh, Hindu, Buddhist, Protestant Christian, Jewish, and Islamic religions. The responsibilities of overseeing a congregation of parishioners are both difficult and challenging. The duties of a chief executive officer are preparing sermons and leading worship services. A career in the clergy professions involves performing religious ceremonies, such as coming-of-age rituals, weddings, and funerals. They are sought for spiritual guidance and other assistance. They promote spirituality and read from sacred texts, share religious insight, and provide faith-based comfort to people. But attending to people with personal and health issues can be overwhelming, and the life-crushing crisis families experience in these times are often catastrophic. The added stress of burying and counseling victims after illness and attacks on their houses of worship are increasing. The administrative cost to the edifice after catastrophic events such as an epidemic, pandemic outbreak, attacks, bombings, or fires is a factor and have become our worldwide new normal. When doctors' reports are not encouraging, financial pressures are increased, or efforts to reconcile relationships fail, all rest on the shoulders of the clergy.

The Needs of Clergy

Many clergy have secondary full-time jobs to support their families, as the day-to-day responsibilities with the added stress and concerns for the safety of worshippers have become increasingly concerning for many in the profession.

Members of the clergy are usually excellent public speakers, good-willing listeners, and often serve others before themselves and their families. They are well educated, prepared, willing to reach out to other communities and countries, and speak more than one language—training may involve reading sacred texts in Arabic, Hebrew, English, or Latin.

Only men can serve as Muslim *imam*s and only unmarried men may serve as priests in most sects of Catholicism. Anglican priests can be women, and married men may serve as Anglican or Eastern Orthodox priests. Each religion has specific processes and requirement for ordaining or appointing members of the clergy, who are willing to make the sacrifices and commitment necessary to serve.

However, the emotional and mental health needs of clergy should be the concern of church hierarchy—bishops, cardinals, and the pope, those in higher authority over houses of worship throughout the diaspora. The days of oversight over the spiritual and religious needs of a congregation alone is a distant bell. The responsibilities of our clergy are now dangerously overwhelming, as their job duties and day-to-day responsibilities have increased significantly. Yet the congregants are dependent upon the heads of houses of worship to oversee and lead in the coordination of all emergency planning and security and safety concerns.

The Selection of and Established Security Committee or Emergency Team Members

One of the initial steps in the process is that clergy and decision makers must choose their security committee or emergency team members and develop their job descriptions. We are fortunate in our congregation because our pastor is qualified and serves in dual roles. He has fire safety officer experience, skills he willingly transferred from his previous denomination. If your leaders possess skills from previous secular activities, this will provide extra support in the planning process.

In addition, we have a well-established trustee board who serves under the supervision of our pastor. Our trustees are responsible for managing church property and overseeing the care and repair of the campus property. The trustees also address the church's long- and short-term needs and goals, in addition to assisting clergy in the management of church resources.

The pastor chose a reverend to lead as vice chair on our board, which was established to apply for state and federal grant funding for the following:

- Feeding programs for the homeless and needy in our community.
- My role as an unpaid volunteer developed into writing the emergency safety and security plan. The plan was needed as a prerequisite for submitting the grant applications for state and federal funding for houses of worship.
- Writing and submitting the application for the governor's safety grants for houses of worship.
- Assist with fundraising and dispersing funds for special projects occurring within the church.

The board members were tasked to meet regularly with our secretary. Minutes and bylaws are kept in our Google Drive. The final draft of our plan, drills, and training documents are archived.

Again, we were fortunate because the head of the trustee board and one trustee member served on the board with me.

Overall, stewardship is a theological belief that humans are responsible for the world and should take care of it and others. In Jewish, Christian, Sikh, Hindu, Buddhist, and Muslim traditions, stewardship refers to the way time, talents, material possessions, or wealth are used or given for the service of God.

In my worship house, the stewards, stewardess, and members of the congregation are active, retired, or employed. Several members on our boards and committees had received active shooter training in their places of employment. The relationship with local Protective Security Advisors were already established. The members decided to invite the local crime prevention specialist to our worship house to teach active shooter training. I had already included this written course in our training plan and I was able to benefit from the police training course as a supplement to our written training plan. Several of our leaders and ministers attended the training with enthusiasm—

it was their idea and they asked good questions. The most important question from my perspective was: When and what will be our next safety and security training and which members would receive the next tier of training? Our vice chair and associate pastor were present. Both were able to respond and assured the congregation of our commitment to follow through. I had already begun writing our church Emergency Operations Safety and Security Plan and I had added the coordinator of church security to my team of experts—including a reverend employed as a local police officer, who volunteered as our active shooter consultant. She was present to offer support of the plan—although the local police department forbade her to use her work title in her worship house.

Identifying Participants for Security Committee or Emergency Team Members

Conduct background checks before hiring staff and volunteers.

Security committees as volunteers are suggested in other worship houses with one individual as the head. The committee should meet regularly (once a month) while the plan is being developed and underway. Regular meetings are suggested during times of crises and during all security-related activities.

It is helpful if the security leader has some law enforcement or emergency management experience or background.

If the scope of the planning process exceeds the academic background of the members, other people may be needed and recruited to participate in the planning process. Select participants based on their extensive knowledge or their importance for successful implementation and completion in all phases of the planning. A diverse group with experience working with or serving the elderly and physically challenged population is suggested.

The members who are willing to carry out the tasks and are proven dependable do not need an extensive academic background to be chosen to serve. Try not to exceed eight or more participants on your security committee. Your ability to come to consensus is jeopardized when there are too many members. You can always invite other participants if specific expertise is needed.

Be sure that every step in the job description process identifies who is to perform specific tasks or duties—rather than names, use their positions, such as senior trustee, children's director, and so on.

Stakeholder Buy-In: Why Is It Important?

From a planning perspective, the stakeholder buy-in was flawless. Unfortunately, it came at a cost—fear and concern. The local news media had reported shooting and physical damages to local churches and synagogues.

Buy-in involves respect and teamwork. Our house of worship's safety and security training plan is nonfinancial. However, we eventually hired armed security. This plan involved acceptance of an idea and need for necessary changes in how we operate to secure our worship house.

In this case, fear, including safety concerns for our congregants and their families, seemed to be the primary motivation. The police trainer shared the uncomfortable truth and it was not what our members wanted to hear. There are negative consequences for lack of stakeholder participation. Our senior leadership was apprised of the necessary planning and training required during a trustee meeting with the clergy. As a result, several attendees volunteered their time, as well as specific academic and professional expertise and talents, to teach various training classes.

I continually reaffirmed our goals and communicated our collective progress throughout the execution of the plan.

A buy-in is necessary when we are implementing change in any project, venue, or houses of worship. We want to avoid pushback, turf power struggles, and acting out behavior, which may occur.

The clergy must reinforce the plan, and the congregation must be confident of the clergy's support in all aspects of the project. To this end, regular meetings with all boards, leadership, and committees are important to promote positive communication and clarify miscommunication and answer questions.

Congregants will only do what makes sense to them to the level they agree with what they are being told or instructed to commit to. It should be for their personal well-being and add value to their lives. It should be for the greater good of all who are involved. Cliques should be avoided at all costs. All congregants should be welcome to participate wherever they are needed at their skill level.

Plan Your Success

Setting Specific and Measurable Goals

Once your team of decision makers (security committee) are assembled, goal setting is your next focus. The ideal approach is brainstorming to capture everyone's or board members' ideas and suggestions regarding the process. What are the main themes or concerns of the brainstorming session? These can form the development of three or four measurable goals that are doable with desired outcomes. There is no point in developing procedures that are impractical and cannot be implemented.

Getting Project Approval and Lessons Learned

The clergy (facility manager) was present, the board was assembled, the goals were set, and a proposed schedule was in place. This was a perfect time for me to get approval from the pastor and board members. The plan I outlined and developed included a mission statement. This tool provided a sound foundation to present additional ideas to leadership and other security team members at the table.

This suggestion will provide a solid foundation to sell your ideas and bring your plan the visibility that will aid in its success.

It is recommended that there be one person in charge in any security chain of command. This person will be responsible for security-related decisions and inspections, the development and reassessment of the security plan, annually or biannually, and ongoing review of the current plan.

You Will Need a Mission Statement

(Forms are available in the "Useful Forms" section.)

The needed mission, vision, and goals will have a positive impact and greatly assist your local communities. Your internal teams and external partners (i.e., law enforcement agencies, community organizations, community presentation specialist, protective security advisors, politicians, and other surrounding community houses of worship) can provide positive feedback and assist with your writing of the planning outline.

Knowing What to Expect

There are common reactions at this point—at least, there were for me. If this is the first project you've planned, you may feel overwhelmed, which is understandable. After all, this is all new. Remember, in God's eyes, you are trying to make a difference in the safety and security of your worshippers. If you plan your success and just take it one step at a time, you will be fine.

That is what this book is all about.

Understanding the Time and Efforts Required

The pitfall I experienced was my not realizing the time commitment needed to complete each module. Estimating is the process of looking into the future and gauging what it will take to do something. Most people like me—especially if they know a little about the subject—tend to underestimate the time commitment or resources required to write and complete a safety and security plan. Perhaps, I should have selected a smaller process. I am fortunate to have an emergency management background and have worked with others who are professional trainers and planners.

If you have access to people who have done this before, use them as a resource. As you gain experience, you will be better equipped to tackle tougher planning processes.

This is an area in which it is better to walk before you run.

Lessons Learned: Understanding What Needs Changing

I backed away from any attempts to write grant applications, as my priorities changed. I decided to continue writing the safety and security plan for the main edifice of the worship house that included the additional building on the campus. I was more effective in my efforts when I decided to concentrate on one major task at a time. Otherwise, I would be torn in too many directions, which would result in broken focus—a kiss of death for any activity or project. I did not have the support of several team members developing the policy and training modules. I completed the document independently. Leadership advised me of what they needed within the plan and discontinued any tangible planning or clerical support.

My customers were members of the clergy and congregation. I communicated with our clergy and board members to solicit feedback and asked what their vision was. At times, they seemed uncertain, so I was left on my own to work independently with books, policies, and checklists.

Limited Authority

(A process mapping form are in the "Useful Forms" section.)

I focused on the tasks as I was on the board, but I was not necessarily on a team. I was given a task with no real authority. This may be problematic at the implementation and training phase of the plan. If you are assigned a task without authority, you are limited in your capacity to further implement the additional steps needed to complete the project. You are at the mercy of other members in your purview.

However, if you are given the project with clearly defined authority, you are a leader. You have the capacity to develop additional guidelines needed to see the operation to fruition and have the room to do the following:

- Work creatively.
- Manage your time.
- Increase and develop specific skills with the persons who are working with you.
- Develop organizational order.

In addition, you could expand the project and develop an organized, focused, and well-trained team.

There will be times and situations when leadership is too busy to assist you. I used my emergency management training and mental health background to power through the writing process—my training in psychology was extremely helpful.

If You Are Working Alone

Determine where you are and what or where your starting point is. Your written outline will be helpful.

A Note of Encouragement for the Readers

Have you felt God's prompting you to do something that seems impossible? What if all you have to do is agree to try? Maybe you dream of accomplishing something but do not believe you can. What if He gave you that dream, and He is just waiting for your prayers and requests for help? Ask for help when you need it.

Work Your Encouragement

How will you overcome the obstacles?
What are your options?
What do you have to lose by trying?
What do you have to gain?
Plan your work and work your plan.
Never be too proud to seek help, wherever it is available.

Chapter 1

If You Fail to Plan,
You Plan to Fail

The Next Step in Planning Is to Lay Out Your Project Plan Outline

(A process mapping form are in the "Useful Forms" section.)

How to Create Your Own Process Map

A process map is a handy tool used by many organizations, like emergency management agencies and planners, to gain a better understanding of your process. It is especially useful when there are complicated plans to examine and write. In this case, the map is an outline or picture of everything that you anticipate happening within your planning process. You might consider, it is often easier to begin at a top level of hierarchy and work your way down to the lower levels of detail. If you are already familiar with your planning process, you may choose to start at a lower level.

As a suggestion, there should be no more than ten tasks at any one level. Simplify your process.

Initially, I followed the suggested text: FEMA's June 2013 *Developing High-Quality Emergency Operations Plans for Houses of Worship* guide. This plan is the standard in most worship houses in the United States. While this is an outstanding publication and many checklists followed, it was necessary for me to deviate and develop a planning process map that addressed the needs of our worship house.

The Plan Content (Where to Begin)

The safety policy is the beginning. A comprehensive safety program should be developed for your organizational needs. A plan should be written to provide a basic outline and overview of your house of worship's operation.

The plan ensures that all who are involved with the house of worship are responsible for implementing the plan and are familiar with its provisions. They should actively participate in its modifications and receive updates each time the plan is changed.

If there are more than one house of worship, each site should have an emergency plan tailored to the locations site needs.

The Purpose and Situation Overview

Review the samples as the purpose sets the foundation for the entire plan. It is a general statement of what the plan is meant to do. The situation overview explains why the plan is necessary.

The Purpose and Scope

The purpose of this document is to outline the process for how your organization will prepare, respond to, and recover from emergencies or disasters. This document will cover:

- ✓ Facility safety assessments
- ✓ Congregation demographics
- ✓ Risk assessment
- ✓ Legal litigation
- ✓ Weather emergencies/natural disasters and threats: floods, tornadoes, and power outages
- ✓ Environmental emergencies/hazardous materials/threats to public health: chemicals in solid, liquid, or gas form; toxic leaks; spills as solid liquid
- ✓ Different levels of emergencies/disasters
- ✓ Roles and responsibilities of staff, congregants, and volunteers
- ✓ Response protocols (for incidents requiring internal and/or external coordination)
- ✓ Criminal acts, bombs, explosions, or domestic and workplace violence
- ✓ Business impact analysis (BIA)

✓ Continuity of Operations Plans (COOP, including health issues)
✓ Security site assessments
✓ Procedures for specific types of emergencies/disasters: fire safety planning, active shooter training, evacuation plans, threat assessments, and specific drills for your worship house, including incident command (ICS), FEMA and Homeland Security Guidelines
✓ Public health emergency planning: epidemics and pandemics

The Situation Overview Statement

Disasters and emergencies can strike any place at any time. An emergency or disaster could have devastating long-lasting impacts on houses of worship in the safest communities everywhere. Impacts could include injury or loss of life, which happened at the Emanuel African Methodist Episcopal Church in Charleston, South Carolina, on June 17, 2015. There were nine fatalities that occurred during this active-shooter incident. African American churchgoers were targeted. The negative emotional impact on congregants, family members, and the nation was devastating.

Other threats are the damage or loss of the facility, damage of equipment or furnishings, loss of personal property, loss of revenue, or loss of donations. To mitigate the potential impacts on sanctuaries and our surrounding community, our house of worship developed this plan as a guide for how we plan to address disasters and emergencies that may impact our edifice, congregants, leadership, or our community.

How a Policy Statement Is Written

The purpose of the emergency preparedness plan (EPP) is to provide a safe and secure environment and campus. The EPP includes parking locations and the immediate surrounding grounds of the edifice. The plan is designed to work toward the elimination or control of all hazards for all building occupants. To accomplish this mission, we must strive to provide a safe and secure place of worship for all congregants and visitors. This document provides an overview of how we plan to address any disaster or emergency that may impact our community.

When to Review the Plan?

The plan will evolve on a continuous basis after it is written and approved for use. It will evolve as lessons are learned. There will be new information, insight, and after-action reporting of drills and exercises. Your worship house should establish a process for reviewing and revising the plan. However, it might be beneficial to review and revise in portions either annually or biannually. Discuss how and when the plan will be changed and specify who has the responsibility for modifying the plan—as a suggestion, the clergy or designee should oversee the implementation and the process.

Sample Document Signature Page

The approval and implementation page introduce the plan. It indicates that it supersedes all previous plans. It gives both the authority and the responsibility to house of worship leadership and designees to perform specific tasks. This document should be signed and periodically updated by leadership. This document should include a date and signature by the house of worship's senior leadership.

(Forms are available in the useful forms section)

Federal Emergency Management Agency Guidelines

Guide for Developing High-Quality Emergency Operations Plans for Houses of Worship, June 2013

Figure 1: Steps in the Planning Process

STEP 1 Form a Collaborative Planning Team	STEP 2 Understand the Situation	STEP 3 Determine Goals and Objectives	STEP 4 Plan Development (Identifying Courses of Action)	STEP 5 Plan Preparation, Review, & Approval	STEP 6 Plan Implementation & Maintenance
Identify Core Planning Team	Identify Threats and Hazards	Develop Goals		Format the Plan	Train Stakeholders
Form a Common Framework	Assess Risk	Develop Objectives		Write the Plan	Exercise the Plan
Define and Assign Roles and Responsibilities	Prioritize Threats and Hazards			Review the Plan	Review, Revise, and Maintain the Plan
Determine a Regular Schedule of Meetings				Approve and Share the Plan	

NOTE: Clergy is the House of Worship Leadership

The above document is the industry standard (the holy grail of emergency management)

Sample layout:

The emphasis will be placed on the following needs of our congregation's written plan:

- Emergency telephone numbers
- Medical emergency
- Shelter in place plan
- Facility evacuation plan

1. Evacuation planning from the sanctuary
2. Evacuation from the sanctuary or campus buildings

3. Evacuation of children, youth, and teachers from house of worship school
4. Evacuation of adults and children from special programs
5. (i.e., feeding programs for the homeless and guests)
6. Evacuation of all guests in the facility

✓ Active shooter plan
✓ Fire safety plan
✓ Training for all disciplines
✓ Drills for all congregants and visitors

CHAPTER 2

COMMON FRAMEWORK THE INCIDENT COMMAND SYSTEM (ICS)

Common Framework the Incident
Command System (ICS)

The framework we will utilize is the Incident Command System (ICS), a standardized approach to the command, control, and coordination of emergency response, by providing a common hierarchy within which our worship house response personnel can be effective in accordance with our skill levels and secular work experiences.

ICS Defined

ICS consists of a Federal Emergency Management System (FEMA)–inspired standard management hierarchy and procedures for managing temporary emergency incidents of any size.

Presidential Policy Directive 8 (PPD-8), which was signed by the president in March 2011, describes the nation's approach to preparedness. This directive represents an evolution in our collective understanding of national preparedness, based on the lessons learned from criminal activities, hurricanes, house of worship incidents, and other experiences. PPD-8 defines preparedness around five mission areas: prevention, protection, mitigation, response, and recovery (which, for the purposes of this guidance, means the capabilities necessary to avoid, deter, or stop an imminent crime, threat, or actual mass casualty incident).

1. Prevention is the action that houses of worship take to prevent a threatened or actual incident from occurring. Protection means the capabilities to secure houses of worship against acts of terrorism and man-made or natural disasters.
2. Protection focuses on ongoing actions that protect people, networks, and property from a threat or hazard.
3. Mitigation means the capabilities necessary to eliminate or reduce the loss of life and property damage by lessening the

impact of an incident. Mitigation also means reducing the likelihood that threats and hazards will happen.

4. Response means the capabilities necessary to stabilize an incident once it has already happened or is certain to happen in an unpreventable way, establish a safe and secure environment, save lives and property, and facilitate the transition to recovery.

5. Recovery means the capabilities necessary to assist houses of worship affected by an incident in restoring their environment.

House of worship procedures will be pre-documented, preestablished, and sanctioned by clergy leadership. Our experienced personnel are well trained, and our congregants will be well trained and receive drills in preparation of any incident.

Our personnel represent various agencies, skills, and are selected because of our ability to meld rapidly into a common management structure with common emergency management terminology or language.

Your Emergency, Safety, and Security Plan Should Emphasize

1. Preparedness: training, exercising (drills), evaluating, and taking corrective actions are the primary components of being and becoming better prepared to respond to all hazards and emergency incidents.

2. Prevention: focuses on preventing human hazards, primarily from natural disasters, terrorist attacks, fires, or physical and biological attacks. Preventive measures are designed to provide more permanent protections from disasters. The emphasis is to reduce the likelihood of the situation occurring or at least minimizing the impact if or when an emergency occurs.

3. Intervention: emphasizes response capability including the coordination, the management of resources, personnel, equipment, and supplies. This provides adequate response during the emergency to contain the situation. The goal is to provide support and safety to the congregants and all that are involved.

4. Recovery: the recovery phase begins immediately after the threat to human life has subsided. Stabilization efforts include counseling or any assistance offered in an attempt to return to some degree of normal operations and activities.

5. Mitigation: is your effort to reduce loss of life and property by lessening the impact of disasters and emergencies. This addresses structural and nonstructural measures taken to limit the impact of disasters and emergencies.

    a. Structural: actions taken to change the characteristics of buildings or the environment. (i.e., raise building elevations, elevating houses in low-lying areas or on beachfront property, removing buildings in flood zone areas, and replacing them with parks).

    b. Nonstructural: adopting or changing building codes.

Roles and Positions Responsibilities: Worship House Leadership in (ICS) Incident Command System Function

The church clergy serves as the chief emergency preparedness officer and incident commander. They and designees are responsible for overseeing the incident response. The ministerial staff, trustees, and others receive orders and written protocols from house of worship select officers who carry out various support functions during any emergency.

Liaison officer: vice chair, board member, primary contact for supporting agencies and representatives from other supporting community or governmental agencies.

Security team: Monitors safety conditions and develops measures for ensuring safety of all congregants and guests.

Clergy or select team members (public information officer role): speaks with the press and functions as primary spokesperson for the church.

Additional support teams: ushers, usher board, class leaders, teachers, and board of trustees and steward board members will have assigned duties.

The Facility Site Assessment: When Should It Be Done?

Active Shooter Trainers or Protective Security Advisors (PSAs) are field-based representatives who work with faith-based organizations and private sectors to assess the local needs for training, information and technical assistance, security surveys, and vulnerability assessments. Law enforcement, fire department, and other first responders will also serve in this capacity.

The local emergency management agency, the crime prevention specialist and the Criminal Investigation Bureau are available to conduct risk assessment vulnerability meetings with the planning team and worship house leadership. They assess the sanctuary and campus facilities to evaluate and discuss vulnerabilities. They make suggestions for equipment, repairs, and areas that need to be addressed (i.e., shrubbery, easy access by criminals, etc.). Afterward, they submit written detailed improvement suggestions and thorough assessments for each building on all campuses.

Limited Financial or Community Security Resources

Financial and trained security resources may be limited. The vulnerability risk assessment should be performed before developing your emergency plan. The clergy and designee may choose to perform their own site vulnerability assessment, using the tool in the forms section. The security committee lead in the worship house could perform this task. This person would inspect the premises and collect data to submit to the clergy and other decision makers on the team. The following questions should be considered:

1. Does a written plan exist and are there security systems in place now?
2. What is the current risk in this worship house based on incidence that have occurred here or in our community (i.e., vandalism, graffiti, burglary, or verbal threats)? Assess your building in the eyes of a possible bad actor or perpetrator.
3. Considering your financial resources (money), which areas can be improved in the immediate or near future to make the building more secure?
4. Assess the gaps in your present safety plan, if available.
5. Reassess your financial goals and priorities.
6. Does your security equipment need updating and is it adequate (i.e., basic alarm)?

Review equipment checklist in future chapters.

Security Assessment Risk and Crime Prevention Guidance

The Risk Assessment Process

Risks are different for each house of worship, community, city, state, and country. There are differences in mountains, rocky mountains, bushes, forests, islands, and rural and urban communities throughout the world. Therefore, the risk assessment should meet the needs of your specific worship house and location.

Emergency, safety, and security plans need to take into consideration the risks and laws governing specific localities.

The Security Committee Role Dwarfs into the Threat Assessment Team

The security committee at this point also becomes the threat assessment team. Their assignment is to gather additional facts regarding the security protocols to be risk assessed and evaluated. Mitigation protocols are important to protect your worship house and surrounding community.

Out of concern for recent worship house shootings in the United States and abroad, my church conducted a specialized active shooter training seminar in December 2018, on our campus facilities. I evaluated the protocols presented by the speaker. My written emergency plan was tailored to the specific needs of our congregation and edifice.

Our plan considered different layers of the security team. The plan included parking lot attendants, greeters, ushers' roles within the sanctuary, and consideration and protection for most of the people involved in security. Consideration was given for our pastors and lay-clergy who may be more vulnerable to attack. The training plan also included procedures for evacuation and lockdown (shelter in place).

I further assessed needed equipment for communication, which may include walkie-talkies and a NOAA-certified weather alert radio. Our board members had developed a robust lighting project and was in the process of installing outside security cameras on the campus. Five cameras were donated for the entire campus and they were installed in designated areas. The local power company provided installation.

Our plan considered how to communicate effectively during any crisis with security, congregation, and local law enforcement as part of our protocol and risk assessment.

CHAPTER 3

SECURITY SITE ASSESSMENT AND CRIME PREVENTION THROUGH ENVIRONMENTAL DESIGN

The Security Site Assessment

Local law enforcement is available in some communities and conduct the comprehensive "Crime Prevention Through Environmental Design" (CPTED) security assessment of houses of worship. This is recommended by the Federal Emergency Management Agency (FEMA) in the United States. The assessment examines the safety, accessibility, and emergency preparedness of houses of worship, buildings, and campus grounds. This includes a review of the physical facility, landscaping, fencing, access control, and comprehensive lighting assessment (if requested). It also includes crime reduction strategy recommendations to enhance both physical and personal security for your worship house, the structural integrity of the buildings, compliance with architectural standards for individuals with disabilities (special needs), and other access and functional needs, which include emergency vehicle access.

There is no absolute methodology that guarantees the protection of all your assets and all types of potential threats. The assessment is designed with the intention to reduce occurrences of criminal and undesirable untoward behavior in and around your campus facilities.

Based on international community data, there is an urgent need for strongly enforced policies and procedures for worship houses. In some instances, the requirements may be enough to provide adequate protection and deterrents. However, some will require updates and enhancements to improve security. It is based on the needs and your budgeted funding to determine how much security is adequate. It is important to remember no amount of security is effective unless it is regularly monitored and maintained.

The security site assessment should include the following:

1. Property location or locations, if more than one
2. Surveyor name
3. Contact person
4. Building function

5. Threat profile: The primary threat potential is from unauthorized persons gaining access to the named house of worship. This also includes burglary, theft, and other criminal activity occurring on the property. This type of breach could result in crimes against persons and property.

Site Assessment Walk-Through (CPTED) Standard Operating Procedure (SOP) or Methodology:

1. What questions you should expect to answer:
    a) Is or is this location not considered a critical infrastructure target for local bad actors, domestic, or international terrorists?
    b) The law enforcement (representative contact) will walk through with clergy or designees around the campus facility. A determination will be made to assess the following:

    ➢ If this location is or (isn't) a free access facility during business hours and times of worship, are the front doors kept locked or unlocked during business hours and times of worship?
    Example reply: This facility is open (Thursdays, Saturdays, etc.)?

    ➢ Is one or more armed security officer working and what are their hours?

    ➢ How many people volunteer their services at this location?

    ➢ Is this facility equipped with a security alarm system with panic technology and CCTV security cameras?

Crime Prevention Through
Environmental Design (CPTED)

CPTED is based on the premise that proper design and effective use of the built environment can lead to a reduction in the opportunity of crime, thus improving the quality of life and reducing fear. The physical design of buildings, access control techniques, natural and formal surveillance, application of lighting, design, and placement of physical barriers; establishing territoriality (ownership); and maintenance will deter offenders.

Access control: This involves allowing specific people with legitimate and approved reasons to enter the facility and keeping out those that do not. It also makes uninvited persons conspicuous by their mere presence. There are various ways to accomplish this goal. Physical barriers such as fencing, landscaping, solid core doors, deadbolt locks with high-security strike plates, intrusion detection, and intercom systems are a few examples of access control methods.

Natural and formal surveillance: This involves placing windows in locations that allow legitimate users to be seen and enable intruders to be observed and reported to police authorities. Surveillance is enhanced by providing adequate lighting and keeping trees, shrubs, and bushes trimmed to avoid bad actors from using them as concealment. Programs such as Neighborhood Watch and Citizens on Patrol are proven target hardening techniques. CCTV (closed-circuit television) have become affordable for both home and commercial use. These systems will provide formal surveillance.

Territoriality: This involves creating a sense of ownership among legitimate users. It alerts the intruder that they are moving from public onto private property. The use of walkways, sidewalks, landscaping, signage, and fencing serve this purpose.

Maintenance: This involves keeping landscaping trimmed, replacing lights that are out, removing trash, making needed repairs on facility, as the most important crime prevention deterrent.

The broken windows theory contends that if one window is broken and not repaired immediately, others will soon follow. A poorly maintained facility invites crime.

Additional Security Equipment for Your Consideration to Improve Safety within Buildings and Grounds

After conducting the facility safety assessments or site visit of all the buildings on the property, a review of building access is recommended. The security committee or threat assessment team and planners are tasked with identifying additional threats during the process. The team members will decide which threats and hazards will be addressed or if additional security equipment and procedures are needed.

Entrance and exits are traditionally left unlocked during worship services for latecomers. Many worship houses rent their facilities for weddings, parties, and businesses that conduct various workshops and training. Staff and volunteers need access to the campus buildings to prepare for events.

All suspicious activity should be reported to the security team or other designees.

A list of additional safety measures your worship house should consider:

1. *Technology-driven panic buttons*: Alarm system companies are normally able to alert multiple responders with a push of a button. They decrease response time during an emergency. This instant notification allows authorities to dispatch first responders the moment an alert is received. There is no hardwiring involved and the setup takes a few minutes. Panic button software programs are relatively inexpensive for some worship houses. Panic alarms can be installed at public reception areas where staff can initiate emergency procedures when needed.

2. *CCTV system video surveillance*: Camera coverage should be considered for critical areas. They can focus on items that are most likely to be stolen. For houses of worship on a limited budget, a camera with audio can be monitored from a cell phone. The purchase price is approximately $300.00.

3. *Alarm system*: Install basic burglar and fire alarm systems. The local fire department can assist your worship house in determining adequate coverage and codes for your campus facility. A camera system can serve as an alarm system using video analytics and integrating with access control systems.

4. *Security alarm system*: This system should be used to monitor and provide coverage throughout the campus by the means of motion sensors. This system can be used to monitor exterior/interior doors and windows. Sensors can be placed around the perimeter of the worship house, within it, or both. Sensors can detect intruders by using various methods, such as monitoring doors and windows for opening or by monitoring unoccupied interiors for motions, sound, vibration, or other disturbances.

Types of sensors most used include:

- broken-glass detection
- inertia
- microwave
- passive infrared
- photoelectric
- smoke, heat, and carbon monoxide detectors
- taut wire fence systems
- ultrasonic
- vibration

The most basic alarm system consists of one or more sensors to detect intruders and an alerting device to indicate intrusion. However, a typical premises security alarm employs the following components:

- Premises control unit (PCU) or panel: The "brain" of the system, it reads sensor inputs, tracks arm/disarm status, and signals intrusions. In modern systems, this is typically one or more computer circuit boards inside a metal enclosure, along with a power supply.
- Alerting devices: These indicate an alarm condition. Usually, these are bells, sirens, and/or flashing lights. Alerting devices serve the dual purposes of warning occupants of intrusion and potentially scaring off burglars. These devices may also be used to warn occupants of a fire or smoke emergency condition.
- Keypads: Small devices, typically wall mounted, which function as the control interface of the system. In addition to buttons, keypads typically feature indicator lights, a small multi-character display, or both.
- Interconnections between components: This may consist of direct wiring to the control unit or wireless links with local power supplies.
- Security devices: Devices to detect thieves such as spotlights, cameras, and lasers.

5. *Computers*: Cybercrime is a prevalent global threat. Ensure all passwords are protected and changed frequently. Use of malware and virus protection is highly recommended. Never leave your computer on or unattended when not in use.

6. *Wi-Fi*: Separate public and private use of Wi-Fi offers control of persons who can access sensitive information over the public network and restrict the security system to private Wi-Fi networks.

7. *Bollards*: When installed properly, they guide traffic and mark boundaries. They come in a variety of shapes and

styles. Bollards can be installed to physically block vehicles and protect both people and property. They are made from metal, stone, cement, or plastic.

8. *Barrier doors*: Doors should be solid wood or metal (with minimal glass) and are only as good as the locks and the door jams that secure them. Locks should be deadbolts installed by a professional locksmith. They should go at least 2.5 or 3 inches into a steel jam. It should not be possible to open the deadbolt by breaking and reaching into a nearby windowpane. If the lock is near a window, it should open with a key, but sliding bolts and hotel-style bar locks can be present for quick securing.

9. *Glass doors*: Doors with excessive glass near them are not recommended. Glass that is tempered bulletproof or Lexan are recommended. Sliding bolts and chains can be used to secure less used doors that are away from the main entrance when the edifice is not in use. Care must be considered in maintaining emergency egress in case of fire or other emergencies in which escape is necessary.

10. *Interlocking door systems*: These systems are site-specific applications used for houses of worship, government, and buildings that can be closed and activated from the inside at the main entrances for use during services. If security spots a dangerous or armed person approaching the worship house, this will hopefully delay the bad actor from entering the main sanctuary or building.

11. *Two-way radios*: Eliminate faulty or spotty cell phone service. Ushers and worship house staff can relay information quickly throughout the campus.

12. *Safe rooms*: The rooms are recommended during active shooter training and incidence. They are preplanned, designated secure rooms and spaces to retreat to, should the worship house or campus come under attack by armed intruders. The room should have solid doors and more

than one exit. Sturdy locks that can be locked from the inside without keys are recommended.

13. *Tornado shelters*: These rooms can be used for weather-related or security situations, depending on their location.

14. *Fencing*: Fencing can be used as a barrier to entry. Although they can be scaled, they act as a deterrent if the bad actor does not want to be detected. The location and type of fencing is site-specific. If fencing is installed, a maintenance program should be implemented to keep the fencing and gates in good repair or operating condition.

15. *Parking lots*: Be observant when entering parking areas and do not leave valuables in vehicles.

16. *Outside landscape*: Landscaping should be coordinated with site lighting. This is recommended to avoid the creation of shadows and difficulty viewing various outdoor areas. Use landscaping, walls, and fences to define the boundaries of the campus, as this gives a sense of ownership. Prune shrubs, bushes, and trees to avoid concealment of bad actors. Worship house visibility of outdoor areas should never be blocked, if possible. Prickly or thorny foliage as a barrier of prickly hedge is recommended near the campus to deter trespassing or concealment—such as wild roses or whichever is prevalent in your specific area or zone.

17. *Lighting*: This is a (CPTED) security feature that meets the industry standards recommended by the *Illuminating Engineering Society of North America*, or your specific location. Lighting is a proven deterrent to intruders and other bad actors and enables detection. Proper lighting is a highly effective crime-control method.

    The laws in various US localities require buildings to maintain adequate lighting.

    The laws are subject to change in your specific location.

18. *Key control locks*: Require employees and staff to turn in keys when transferred, terminated, or retired. Keys that are issued to nonemployees or volunteers should be tracked

and turned in when applicable. These keys should be of a nonduplication type. Keys should never be transferred from one user to another without audit and new documentation. Stamp keys do not duplicate. This does not mean keys cannot or will not be duplicated. Do not permit keys, particularly masters, to be taken home. Require keys to be signed in and signed out in a daily log, especially to subcontractors or day users of the campus facility, when practical. Rotate locks when applicable. Locks should be changed periodically.

Locks should be patented keyway or electronic means that will not allow for unauthorized duplication.

19. *Safes*: Keep a record of locations of safes and their combinations. Safes should be burglar and fire-resistant. Safes containing cash or other valuables should have locks with individual combinations and audit trail capabilities. Install electronic access control locks or fully mechanical, push button combination access control locks (commonly referred to as cipher locks) to rooms that contain valuable equipment.

Contract with an experienced and *certified* locksmith who understands the needs of worship houses.

CHAPTER 4

DISASTER PREPAREDNESS

Disasters from Another Perspective

1. A crisis is defined as an unforeseen situation. The situation is or can be classified as a disaster, catastrophic threat, or urgency.

    •   Disasters are classified into two categories: man-made and natural.

2. Man-made disasters are classified as terror attacks, chemical accidents, oil spills, hazmat spills, sabotage, or other consequential actions caused by human beings.

    •   Global warming can be included in this category; technological advances such as bio-nuclear terrorism, explosions, hacking, and communication system breakdowns
    •   The Deepwater Horizon oil spill in the Gulf of Mexico in 2010
    •   The Flint Michigan water crisis in 2014

3. Natural disasters are classified as natural events: earthquakes, floods, droughts, tornadoes, and hurricanes.

    •   Hurricane Katrina was a category 5 hurricane that made landfall in Florida and New Orleans, Louisiana, in 2005, and caused 1200 deaths in New Orleans. The flooding was caused by fatal engineering flaws in the flood protection system known as levees.
    •   Pandemics can be considered the worst natural disasters. They can begin as a flu or virus and evolve from an epidemic that spreads and causes the death of hundreds of thousands of people throughout the world.

4. The size of the disaster emergency is important.

    •   If the emergency is small, they are mere hazards or
        incidents and local emergency managers can handle
        the response. If it is a moderately sized disaster that
        leads to loss of life and property, then the disaster is
        not within the control of the local level, and additional
        state and federal support is called upon.

House of Worship Staff
Responsibilities and Suggestions

Before and During Each Service or Event

Take a head count as ushers, trustees, stewards, class leaders, or security should be assigned to take an "at time of service or an event
head count." Assign someone to conduct a walk-through to ensure
everyone is safe.

Hall Monitor Guidance

1. Introduce yourselves to the security officer on duty.
2. Patrol throughout the house of worship buildings and
    campus.
3. Check restrooms regularly.
4. Close and lock doors and turn off lights when classrooms
    are not in use.
5. Check choir rooms or closets.
6. Check kitchen and fellowship areas.
7. Survey the parking lots for suspicious activities.
8. Approach and engage persons wandering throughout the
    building and campus, especially during worship services
    and other events.
9. Be wary of strangers claiming to be visiting clergy, students
    of architecture, or anyone who is curious about the facili-

ties and campus. Do not be shy about asking for identification as bona fide visitors will be willing to provide it.

Additional Security Guidance

1. Keep lights on inside of the edifice. This may deter someone from breaking in and allow passersby to observe if one does occur.
2. Signs and exterior crosses and religious displays should be unbreakable, with individual lighting.
3. Special displays, such as nativity scenes, should be well lit and securely fastened to the ground.
4. Special items, such as worship objects, artifacts, and silver historic items that are of value, require special attention, should be insured—a strong security plan may reduce insurance costs. If the lists of items are not secured, do not describe or advertise them. This could provide information to those with criminal intent.
5. Inspect the whole facility, including the final check of all restrooms, before locking up.
6. Keep announcements of a clergy's absence to a minimum. Bad actors often look for these announcements in the newspaper, church bulletin boards, or social media. They are a tip-off that the building may be unattended.
7. *The main sanctuary*: The main worship area and other areas on campus used for worship should be maintained in a safe and secure manner during and between use. The emergency response options and protocols should be known by designated responsible designees. In the event of emergencies, the sanctuary should be evaluated for hazards, maintenance issues, exits in case of emergency, and areas of protection.

8. *Money collection*: A protocol should be established that ensures safe and secure protocols for handling cash, checks, credit card accounts, and cash app accounts.
Safe storage and transporting of funds to bank and immediate accounting of all funds.
9. If you see or hear suspicious activity, report all observations to the security team or other designees.
10. Exercise additional common sense monitoring duties as assigned or needed.

Facility Closing Protocol

Official closing of house of worship for unscheduled reasons, such as emergencies, regular services, special activities, and closings during church office hours will be ordered by clergy or the following designees:

_____
_____
_____
_____
_____

Communicating with Local Media

Media Communications (Forms are available in the "Useful Forms" section)

Media Communications (Emergency Action):

Because emergencies may attract media attention, employees and congregants are to direct all media inquiries they receive to clergy or designees:

_____
_____
_____
_____
_____

Public Information Officer

Media Communications (Forms are available in the "Useful Forms" section)

Only one public information officer is needed; however, the clergy may designate others who will interact with the media in his or her absence.

The duties include the following:

Provide reliable information to staff, visitors, and families.

Give information and respond to media inquiries.

Establish a Joint Information Center (JIC) or staging areas for the media.

Interact with local government, law enforcement, and emergency responders. **Templates samples titled "How to Address the Media and How to Write a Press Release" are in the "Useful Forms" section of this book. Personnel will not have to compose them during the confusion and chaos during any emergency event.

Communication with External Community Partners

It is important to address beforehand how the worship house will communicate with all the individuals who are directly or indirectly involved in the emergency or crisis. Plan how to communicate with families, community members, and the media.

When to Keep Community Partners and the Media Informed

Be clear about what steps have been or should be taken to attend to member safety after the crisis event. Inform families and community members what support services the facility is providing, or what other community resources are available. This information sharing should be the responsibility of clergy or designees responsible for public or media relations.

Develop Ongoing Positive Relationships with Law Enforcement Agencies in Your Community

Collaborative planning teams should be an active part of the process in the development of your emergency plan. They should be professionals with varied expertise (i.e., law enforcement, emergency management, fire and medical personnel, mental health professionals, and various religious organizations within your community). I cannot stress this enough.

Civil Rights Advocates, Elected Officials, and Attorneys

Advocacy community partners should be available and include emergency call down lists, cell phone lists, and Rolodex to coordinate with Muslim, Arab, African American, Jewish, Sikh, and other targeted minorities, especially groups who have been subject to harassment, hate crimes, and discrimination.

Regular meetings should be coordinated with interfaith and minority groups. These meetings should focus on building lines of communication and support as to how they address issues of discrimination and bigotry.

CHAPTER 5

PREPARING FOR AN EMERGENCY

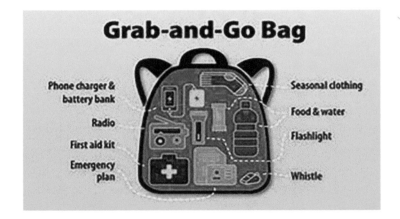

Emergency Guidelines and Preparation for Disasters and National State of Emergency

1. It is recommended that worship houses should conduct fire drills, first aid, CPR training, and evacuation drills annually.
2. Ensure two or more of the following are in place: telephone tree, Twitter, Facebook, e-mail, text messaging, or other social media in place for officers, ministerial staff, class leaders, and members.
3. Head count of designees, ushers, trustees, stewards, class leaders, or security should be assigned to take an "at time of service, program, or religious classes" head count. This should include names of attendees during epidemic or pandemic for needed contact tracing.
4. Assign someone to conduct a walk-through to ensure everyone is safe.
5. Designees, stewards, and trustees should review and explain the location of exits in bulletins, at conferences (meetings), and with new members.
6. Designated staff should have CPR and AED training for nursing units and departments.

Ensure the following items are always available:

> List: portable radio, batteries, hand-crank radio, flashlights, toilet paper, box of trash can liners, handy-wipes, paper towels, heavy-duty tape, plastic tarps, first aid kits, fire extinguishers (inspected annually and training updates), personnel first aid kits, disposable gloves, masks, AED equipment, female supplies, blankets, water, orange emergency cones, and bleach. Ample trash cans or buckets with bleach can work as toilets.

Ensure important documents are in waterproof containers. All keys and codes are available to designated staff.

Recommend all clergy and designated staff carry in your vehicle or store in your office the following:

> List: masks, comfortable clothing, sturdy shoes, socks, first aid kit, prescription medication, healthy snacks, water, and reading material *(cell phone and charger added).*

Additional Recommendations and Guidelines

(Additional information and forms are included in the "Continuity of Operation," "Business Impact Analysis," and "Useful Forms" sections.)

A secure on- or off-site location is needed to store the following:

> Original or duplicate copies of accounting records, legal documents, staff and congregants' contact information—adult and children with alternate contact information—including other essential records.

Establish a plan to resume worship services:

> Consider providing worship services through several communication venues, such as telephone ministry, e-mail, internet, schools, and social media platforms. Preestablish alternative reciprocal agreement relocation services with other facilities in case of emergencies.

Additional needs considerations:

> Persons with pets, persons with disabilities, persons living in poverty, persons with children and single-parent households. All should be considered in shelter in place and evacuation protocols (i.e., before evacuating your home, put a secure alert sticker on your door to alert emergency crews if your pet is inside).

Medical staff training:

> Include first aid procedures, including protection against blood-borne pathogens and respiratory protection.

There are further areas to consider in plan development:

1. Ensure there are plans in place for various issues and emergencies that could occur.
2. Emergencies that impact your entire congregation:

   - These are incidence that could affect the entire membership. As outlined as previous risk assessment and emergencies, your worship house should consider the following: events that result in loss of property, structural damage, medical emergencies, theft, arrest, suits, scandals, or death of those in leadership.
   - In case of any internal emergency, anticipate issues that could occur and include various scenarios in your planning process—for example, consider appointing leaders who can work in an acting capacity until a full-time leader is appointed.

3. National emergencies:

- Events like September 11, 2001, which impacted the entire United States and population. Houses of worship were called upon to respond on a dime and offer aid, shelter, and various response efforts within their communities.

Why You May Need a Business Impact Analysis (BIA) and a Continuity of Operations Plan (COOP)

As an addendum to your emergency operations plan, conduct a business impact analysis (BIA) to address the following questions:

1. What procedures are in place if your house of worship, campus, and/or community are rendered inactive because of a disaster, either natural or man-made?
2. What are your alternative plans if your staff are unable to do their work?
3. What if you have no way of reaching your congregants?
4. What are your critical operations?
5. Assess which operations are critical to recovery. Determine which staff, materials, supplies, procedures, and equipment are necessary to maintain operations until the worship house is up and running.
6. Identify all your programs and outreach ministries.

    Congregant prayer and sabbath services, religious instruction, study groups, community programs (i.e., soup kitchen, Alcoholic Anonymous meetings, Boy or Girl Scouts, weddings, and use of meetings and classrooms) on all campuses.
7. Which operations are critical to your survival and recovery?

    Include emergency payroll, financial, and accounting systems. Establish procedures for succession of management (include one individual who is not located at the house of worship). The use of telework enables congregations to continue functioning through any emergency or hazard. This includes any event that would result in closing the house of worship and facilities.

8. Identify programs that are critical to your worship facility.

Prioritize the programs you have identified and decide which are critical and need to function quickly during the post-disaster period. An example is worship services.

Inventory the separate processes that allow each critical program to function. For example, to run your soup kitchen, you must do the following:

- Pay employees to coordinate volunteers.
- Continue your access to food and other supplies.
- Ensure you have a facility to work out of.
- Conduct outreach to community and customers.

You have already conducted your risk assessment and impact analysis as part of the emergency plan. Plan for how you will communicate with staff during an emergency, include congregants who must evacuate the area (out of state, county) and edifice.

Develop this crisis management procedure in advance and update, review, and conduct drills with tabletop exercises and the emergency plan—at least annually—to ensure the plan addresses various, if not all, scenarios.

CHAPTER 6

BUSINESS INTERRUPTION INSURANCE

Why Business Interruption Insurance Is Important

Insurers knew the damage a viral pandemic could wreak on businesses, but they decided to exclude coverage. Lessons learned from the 2002–3 SARS outbreak led insurance companies to exclude coverage for many of the losses suffered today by business. Some industry watchers predict a tidal wave of litigation over whether policies should cover losses due to the coronavirus closures. SARS, which infected eight thousand people mostly in Asia and is now seen as foreshadowing the COVID-19 pandemic, led to millions of dollars in business interruption insurance claims.

As a result, many insurers added exclusions to standard commercial policies for losses caused by viruses or bacteria. Other types of insurance policies may still have to pay out. Personal travel and event cancellation policies are expected to face huge claims from the 2019–20 coronavirus pandemic, according to industry reports.

Few successful claims are expected to come from traditional business insurance lines because of the exclusion of virus-related damages.

Insurance disputes caused by coronavirus shows the need for a government-supported solution, such as a national pandemic insurance program, like the National Flood Insurance Program.

To date, about one-third of US businesses have "business interruption insurance," which is intended to cover losses from an event that forces companies to suspend or stop operations.

Many policies also have "civil authority" clauses that cover losses when a governmental agency stops a business from operating. A common example would be a fire that damages a restaurant and leads the fire marshal to close it down.

Do Houses of Worship Operate as Businesses?

Why Worship Houses Are Considered a Business in the Insurance Industry

Business interruption insurance is not sold as a separate policy. It is either added to a property/casualty policy or included in a comprehensive package policy as an add-on or rider.

What happens if your worship house is damaged and can no longer function? What if the worship house is harmed by a fire, flooding, tornado, or vandals? Your congregation could lose its place of worship, its sources of income, and its ability to serve the community.

Many worship houses have property insurance that protects in the event of a loss. Not all worship houses buy business interruption insurance. With this insurance, you would receive money to compensate for your loss of incoming donations and tuition. If you must shut down operations, this coverage could protect your worship house and other campus facilities for a myriad of reasons.

What Exactly Is Business Interruption Insurance?

1. Business interruption insurance provides coverage that replaces business income lost in a disaster.
2. This insurance also covers operating expenses, payroll taxes, and loan payments.
3. It covers a move to a temporary location, as a part of your business continuity and continuity of operations plan.
4. Business interruption insurance also applies if the government mandates a shutdown of nonessential businesses or operations to cease temporarily.
5. The insurance premiums or the additional cost of the rider is tax deductible, as a business expense.

What Does Business Interruption Insurance Cover?

1. With profits based on prior months' performance, a policy will provide reimbursement for profits that would have been earned had the event or disaster not occurred.
2. Fixed costs include operating expenses and other incurred cost of doing business.
3. For a temporary location, the costs involved with moving to and operating from a temporary business location.
4. Commission and training cost caused by the business interruption. A congregation will often need to replace machinery and retrain personnel on how to use it. The rider might cover these costs.
5. Extra expenses as reimbursement for reasonable expenses beyond the fixed costs. This could allow the worship house to get back on its feet.
6. Civil authority closures that are government mandated and cause financial loss, such as curfews or street closures that are related to the covered emergency event.
7. Employee wages that are essential to the operation of the worship house staff or employees (i.e., man the telephones, make payroll).
8. Tax bills to be paid on time to avoid penalties.
9. Loan payments to be paid while the worship house is not generating income.

The Need to Hire an Attorney

In previous and upcoming chapters, I suggest the worship house consult with and maintain a relationship with an attorney for liability and all business or complex insurance issues. The main lesson learned during the coronavirus and SARS outbreaks is that insurance claims can be denied.

French Court Orders AXA to Pay Restaurant's COVID-19 Business Interruption Losses.

AXA Vows to Appeal

REUTERS, May 22, 2020, by Elizabeth
Pineau and Maya Nikolaeva

A Paris court ruled that insurer AXA must pay a restaurant owner two months' worth of Coronavirus-related revenue losses, the restauranteur's lawyer said on Friday, potentially opening the door to a wave of similar litigation. The ruling will be of interest to restaurants, cafes and nightclubs in Britain and the United States which are also threatening legal action against insurers who have not paid out on business interruption policies.

AXA said it would appeal.

The case was brought by Stephane Manigold, who owns four Paris restaurants. He filed a lawsuit demanding AXA cover his operating losses after a government order in mid-March to close bars and restaurants to slow the spread of the coronavirus. When he learned of Friday's verdict at his office, Manigold high-fived a colleague and his supporters applauded. This is a collective victory," he told Reuters. He later cried as he spoke to reporters in front of one of his shuttered restaurants.

The court said the administrative decision to close the restaurant qualified for insurance cover as a business interruption loss.

This means that all companies with the same clause can appeal to the insurers, Manigold's lawyer, Anais Sauvagnac, said.

AXA said a small number of its clients in the French hospitality sector were covered for

COVID-19 related losses because, they bought a special policy. But most clients in the sector did not have that policy and did not qualify for compensation, AXA said.

If all COVID-19 related losses were deemed covered by insurance, French insurers would have to compensate 20 billion euros ($21.8 billion) per month, industry estimates show.

Whatever the outcome in AXA's court case, prolonged legal wrangling might prompt the French insurance regulator to insist insurers put aside additional reserves to offset legal risk, said Benjamin Serra of Moody's rating agency.

This, Serra said, "would impact insurer' profitability this year."

CHAPTER 7

PUBLIC HEALTH EMERGENCY PLANNING

Public Health Emergency Planning Guidance

There are health issues that may impact the congregants and the community.

Different Levels of Diseases and How the Community Can Be Impacted

1. Epidemic: a widespread occurrence of an infectious disease in a community (i.e., flu epidemic). It spreads quickly and affects many.
2. Pandemic: a disease prevalent over a whole country or the world. A pandemic occurs over a wide geographic area and affects a high proportion of a population.
3. A global epidemic: an epidemic that spreads to more than one continent.

   How is an epidemic different from a pandemic?

   • A pandemic is a bigger epidemic. There is a minor difference between epidemic and a pandemic. An epidemic is where there are numerous breakouts of a single disease.
   • A pandemic is when the disease starts to spread on a larger scale than an epidemic.
   • A pandemic is essentially a bigger epidemic.

4. Endemic: a disease that is constantly present in people of a certain class or in people living in a particular location (i.e., endemic diseases are malaria, hepatitis B infection, and the HIV epidemic although it is starting to be under control in large parts of Africa).

Common Source of Outbreaks

The Centers for Disease Control (CDC) separates outbreaks of disease by the source.

Classification:

1. Pandemic flu or influenza is a respiratory virus that spreads easily from person to person through coughing and sneezing. It can cause mild to severe illness including death. A pandemic flu is caused by a virus that is new to the population or has not circulated recently and widely in the human population. While not all people will become infected during a pandemic, nearly all people are susceptible to infection.

   Various diseases have regularly appeared, which resulted in widespread and community illness, disruption, and death. The Spanish flu of 1918 infected between 25 to 30 percent of the world population and killed an estimated forty to fifty million people.

   The last pandemic was the 2009 H1N1 influenza epidemic, and neither SARS, MERS, nor Ebola qualified as a pandemic despite differing severity, case counts, and death rates. HIV/AIDS is an example of one of the most destructive global pandemics in history. The most recent is COVID-19 in 2019–20, classified as a worldwide pandemic.

2. Communicable diseases or propagated outbreaks are infectious diseases that spread from person to person or from animals to people, including: salmonella, coronavirus (COVID-19) that originated in Wuhan, China, in 2019 (i.e., sharing needles or in cases of Lyme disease by deer ticks).

3. Foodborne/waterborne illnesses disease outbreaks can come from a common source—example, a group of people ate at the same restaurant at the same time and now they have

food poisoning. While common, this is a preventable public health problem. Each year, one in six Americans get sick by consuming contaminated foods and beverages. There are many disease-causing substances, microbes, pathogens, chemicals, and other substances that cause foodborne disease or illness, including *salmonella* and *staphylococcus.*

Why Immunizations Are Important

An immunization is a vaccine, a shot, or a set of shots. They are administered to children at different ages to keep them from developing dangerous and debilitating childhood diseases, i.e., pertussis/whopping cough, polio, measles, chickenpox, and tetanus. They are effective in preventing diseases.

Non-Pharmaceutical Interventions (NPIs) to Reduce Risk

NPIs are actions apart from getting vaccinated and taking medication. If community-spread virus occurs, there should be efforts put in place to contain it. Community-spread virus is often a trigger to begin implementing new strategies tailored to the needs of local circumstances. The goal is to blunt the impact of disease and slow the spread of the virus. There are practical measures (interventions) that can help limit exposure by reducing face-to-face contact in community settings.

1. For schools, options include dividing students into smaller groups, or in severe pandemic outbreaks, closing schools and using internet-based tele-schooling to continue education.
2. For adults, businesses can replace in-person meetings with video or telephone conferences and increased teleworking options.
3. On a larger scale, communities and cities may need to modify, postpone, or cancel mass gatherings.

4. Individuals should stay at home when they are sick.
5. Immunizations are a safe and effective way to gain protection against various communicable diseases.
6. Handwashing often using soap and hand sanitizer with proven techniques.
7. Keep surfaces clean using disinfectant.
8. Masks may be recommended in public settings and help prevent spreading virus or disease to others.

The Congregation Plan for Closure and Teleconferencing

The worship houses should consider plans for church and school dismissals or closures. This could be cancellations, closure, and staff considerations for telework. Houses of worship and associated universities and daycare facilities on campus. All activities and work could be handled remotely to avoid infecting others. There are members in the congregation who may be vulnerable (i.e., senior citizens, medically fragile congregants with preexisting conditions, the disabled and young).

Essential personnel as outlined in the Continuity of Operations Plan (COOP) should be identified in the planning process.

- Who are essential personnel?
- Who needs to report to work?

Civil Liberties Perspective

**There will be civil liberties and liability issues associated with identifying and managing carriers of diseases. This complicates enforcement in all areas of the population including houses of worship.

Conference Options List

1. Teleconference: Is a telephone meeting among two or more participants involving technology more sophisticated than a simple two-way phone connection.
2. Audio conference: At its simplest, a teleconference can be an audio conference with one or both ends of the conference sharing a speaker phone.
3. Video conferencing: Supports the conference by providing video so you can see the person when you are listening to the communicator.
4. Group video call: Using your iPhone, Skype, Snapchat, Facebook Messenger, FaceTime, and Google Hangouts. There can be at least thirty-one users—plus you—in a group, but keep in mind that only the first thirty-one will be able to join. There are limits for iPad, iPhone, or iPod Touch users.
5. Zoom video conferencing: Invite or schedule people to live-video-conference and share a screen.

Standard Universal Precautions

1. Frequently wash your hands with soap and water or alcohol-based hand rub.
2. Coughing and sneezing etiquette: sneeze into the folded arm, cover your cough.
3. Maintain social distancing: depending on the environment, maintain at least six to eight feet between yourself and other people.
4. Avoid close contact with those who cough or are sniffling.
5. If you develop a cough and experience changes in your breathing, seek medical attention early and share your medical and travel history with your health-care provider.
6. Avoid open markets and direct contact with animals and animal products.

7. Careful food safety practices are: well-cooked food, clean produce, pasteurized milk.
8. Do not avoid flu, pneumonia, and other recommended vaccines according to medical diagnosis and age.
9. Avoid travel to endemic areas—there is a World Health Organization (WHO) travel advisory against specific areas.

The Need for a Separate Public Health Planning Ministry

Every congregation should have an emergency preparedness plan that addresses public health emergencies. However, a separate program is not always necessary. This ministry can be integrated into the current preparation planning.

These programs are easier to maintain when they are a part of the overall emergency planning-and-training process.

Public health training can be included for clergy, lay leaders, existing certified medical staff, and volunteers seeking additional skills, including certification with organizations such as American Red Cross for CPR and AED courses on sight or in the current nursing units. The goal is to have a cadre of well-trained volunteers in place that can be called upon when a natural disaster or public health emergency strikes.

If you are a larger congregation with available resources—such as space, food, and money—you may consider providing additional training opportunities for your congregation or surrounding community. The coursework would include how to prepare for both natural and public health disasters (i.e., epidemics and pandemics).

Select a vulnerable group that you wish to serve, such as senior citizens, nursing homes, shelters, or vulnerable people, within your congregation or community.

Assessment in Public Health Emergency Planning

1. Conduct a separate public health risk assessment for the congregation. The assessment tool is provided in the useful form section.
2. Assessment risk is an important task in both emergency and public health planning.
3. Discuss and describe past and anticipated public health emergencies that occurred in your congregation and community. Your awareness can help identify and prepare for future threats to include in your plan.
4. The threats should be ranked from most likely to least likely.
5. Include areas in which sanitation is an issue.
6. Include at-risk members of the congregation, such as the elderly, people with chronic medical or preexisting conditions, families (or single parents) with small children, and the disabled.

Summary Statement

If congregations and their faith leaders never discuss or train in disaster preparedness—GOKITS, evacuation plans, preparedness for pandemics, safe practices regarding not spreading the flu at events—it will jeopardize the health and wellness of congregants, their staff, and communities going forward.

This chapter hopefully gives insight and awareness regarding what we can do to prepare our worship houses.

*   It is not a matter of *if* a health emergency (outbreak) will occur; it is *when*.

Chapter 8

Fire Safety in Churches

Fires can start from natural causes, but many of them are man-made—gas leaks, forest fires, kitchen, trash can, or electrical fires.

Staff Responsibilities During the Fire Emergency

- The following instructions are for designated staff who are assigned to assist in the evacuation of building occupants.
- It is important to remember to assist only when it is safe.
- In the event of fire, staff should use their own judgment in deciding how safe it is to provide help or aid.

1. In the event of being advised of fire or hearing the fire alarm, ensure the alarm has been sounded. The clergy, security, or designated persons should immediately contact the local fire department by calling 911 or whatever is appropriate in your community.
2. Give the name and address of the building and telephone number.
3. Designated staff should meet the fire first responders, explain the situation, and apprise them of the steps that have been taken in accordance with the fire safety plan (i.e., the congregation are all evacuated).
4. Ushers or designees should immediately move vulnerable populations and wheelchairs to safe preplanned areas away from the edifice or campus.
5. The trustees, stewards, ushers, teachers, clergy, or designated layperson will immediately direct all individuals to *exit* buildings using the preplanned evacuation routes and move away from the edifice or campus.
6. After all individuals have been cleared from the bathrooms and meeting rooms, close all doors behind you to the immediate area of the fire to help isolate the smoke and fire. *Do not lock* the doors.
7. If possible, mark all doors after clearing the rooms.

8. Report to clergy or designees after all rooms are clear.
9. Notify the law enforcement or fire first responders if anyone is missing during the emergency.
10. After the response and recovery operation, invite the fire department (first responders) to attend the after-action meeting for debriefing and give them a copy of the emergency safety and security plan—if they don't have one already.

National Fire Protection Guidance: Fire Safety Planning

US Assessment Data for Worship House Campuses:

Main Sanctuary:

- Type of construction
- Access
- Keys
- Location of portable fire extinguishers
- Fire alarm system and panel locations
- Location of exit signs
- Smoke barrier system (e.g., fire doors, utility chases)
- Detection devices (e.g., heat, smoke, or flame detectors; local or central station system)
- Emergency lighting and power
- Heating system
- Fire exits (locations)
- Means of egress
- Evacuation routes
- Stairwells
- Safe rooms for area refuge
- Maintenance schedule
- Maintenance definition
- Fire department access

Additional Buildings:

- Type of construction
- Heating system
- Fire exits (locations)
- Evacuation routes
- Stairwells
- Doors: post signs on permanently closed doors
- Elevators: ensure the elevators are not used during emergencies and drills
- Smoke barrier system (e.g., fire doors, utility chases)
- Detection devices (e.g., heat, smoke, or flame detectors, local or central station system)
- Floor plan maps/fire evacuation diagram: ensure a map of the church with exits is clearly marked and posted on all floors, near stairs, and elevators. Ensure all exits are clear and free of clutter.

Fire Safety Reminders before New Construction and during Renovations

Prior to beginning your new house of worship, addition, or renovation, take time to learn common fire hazards and how to avoid them. When the house of worship construction is completed, learn the details about how to conduct annual fire safety with your team. Be sure to have your evacuation plan in place and schedule fire safety inspections with your local fire department.

The guidance during construction:

1. Follow your local legal requirements for the minimum height of the building numbers to ensure visibility. Building numbers should be large enough to be read from the street. Your local fire department need to easily be able to read all signs on your buildings.
2. Emergency exits should be properly illuminated within the campus buildings.

3. Mark fire extinguishers clearly and make sure they are easily accessible.
4. Clearly mark all electrical control panels.

Identify and Document All Occupants Who Will Use All Campus Facilities

(Adult and children occupants utilize the buildings):

- Clergy, offices, and meeting rooms
- All regularly scheduled and evening services, other miscellaneous classroom meetings
- Adult school and meetings
- Children's school and classes
- Visitors' and congregants' great room parties for dining, meetings, and gatherings

Emergency Call-Down List: (Update this information for newly hired staff or volunteers)

- Clergy and designees: (name and contact information)
- Additional backup persons (names and contact information):

  _____

  _____

- *In* and *out* board or technology to confirm who is on-site in case of emergency:
- (Walkie-talkies, or home/cell phone numbers):

  _____

  _____

Fire Safety Responsibilities

Your responsibility during emergency situations is to know and understand our fire safety plan developed for this campus.

The clergy or designee is the fire safety leader (or designate) or member of an outside emergency service agency who will oversee all safety protocols. Your cooperation may save lives.

1. During an evacuation or emergency, stay calm and follow the emergency protocol plan.
2. As circumstances dictate, the plan may suddenly change, so follow the direction of the safety leader (or designate), or that of a member of an outside emergency service agency. They are trained to serve and protect you and need your cooperation to do so.
3. Fire drills should be held monthly, biannually, or annually, and the clergy or designee will always ensure that the congregation is notified in advance.
4. The purpose of a fire drill is to ensure that the occupants and staff are familiar with emergency evacuation procedures, resulting in orderly evacuation with efficient use of exit facilities.

Conduct Regular Fire Inspections

The fire safety plan should be approved during the inspection by your area or local fire department.

1. Fire evacuation diagrams and maps of the worship house and campus with exit signs are required by law in most jurisdictions to be posted throughout each building and on all floors at visible prominent locations.
2. Train and educate all staff and familiarize them with the locations of the nearest fire hydrants and alarms.
3. Educate staff where the nearest fire station and police station are located and what number to call in your area (i.e., in the United States, call 911).

4. *Keys*: The master keys for the fire department are located _____, and *keys* and *codes* are available to designated staff by name and title.

Location of Alarm Station, Exits, and Extinguishers

Fire Alarm Stations

There is usually a *red* fire alarm signal box at designated marked areas within the edifice (in the United States).

Exits:
Administration and leadership need to know locations of the designated floor plans and exits.

- Portable fire extinguishers dry type—abc
- Stationary fire extinguisher system

Example:
FIRE SAFETY DESIGNEE (Rabbi Jacob Cohen) or another designee, NAME_____.

All staff and congregants should be trained and familiar with the locations of fire extinguishers.

Portable Fire Extinguisher Locations

Place fire extinguishers in plain view and in convenient and accessible locations.

- There are ( ) portable fire extinguishers in the main sanctuary building.
- There are ( ) portable fire extinguishers in all campus locations.

- Train staff, congregants, and volunteers the locations of and how to use fire extinguishers.

  (Familiarize yourself and designees with hallway fire exits, alarms, and extinguishers).
- There are ( ) emergency exits within the buildings.
- Ensure all exits are clear and free of clutter that may impede persons who need to exit the campus during an emergency.
- Fire extinguishers should be regularly tested by a professional.
- The fire system should be tested annually.
- The buildings are equipped with smoke detectors and should be tested on a regular basis.
- Test the sprinkler system weekly or regularly.
  DATE: _____.
- Store materials less than eighteen inches below the ceiling sprinkler heads.

Emergency Lighting and Power

Evaluate and eliminate electrical hazards:

1. Ensure that all exit lighting is operational. Check batteries and light bulbs often.
2. Regularly inspect electrical components for any deterioration.
3. Ensure electrical switches and outlets have properly secured cover plates.
4. When using extension cords for decorative lighting, take them down after the holidays or event to prevent fires.
5. Hire only a certified electrician when electrical maintenance is necessary.

General Housekeeping of Custodial Storage Areas

Utilize proper storing and use of flammable materials, oily rags, and liquids—including cleaning chemicals.

1. Ensure proper storage of gasoline, engines, and equipment (i.e., lawn mowers).
2. Remove all obstacles from hallways, corridors, and rooms that may impede exiting buildings on the worship house campus.
3. Limit the amount and safely use electric cords and adapters throughout the house of worship.

Waste Disposal

1. Provide appropriate trash receptacles for the campus buildings and be sure they are emptied regularly.
2. Keep outdoor trash cans at a safe distance from the buildings.

Main Sanctuary

Buildings on house of worship campus.

Elevator Guidance

1. Identify all public and nonpublic access elevators.
2. Ensure all exit lighting is operational.
3. Ensure the elevators are *not* used during emergencies.
4. Assign trustees, security, or other designated staff to assist persons with wheelchairs and chairlift during an emergency.

Inform emergency personnel if anyone is stuck in the building stairwells.

Fire Extinguishing, Control, or Confinement

RACE Fire Response Procedure: Staff Training Procedure

You must follow the RACE fire procedure before attempting to extinguish a fire.

1. Rescue/remove: Rescue or remove any persons from the immediate scene.
2. Alert/activate: Pull the nearest alarm and call 911—or other in your community.
3. Confine: Close all doors to the hazard/fire area.
4. Extinguish: Extinguish using the closest fire extinguisher if the fire does not impede your ability to evacuate.
5. Evacuate to your designated meeting location.

Use the proper fire extinguishers to fight the fire if there is no additional danger to yourself.

Large Fire:

1. Do not attempt to extinguish big fires.
2. Sound the alarm and immediately call 911—or number in your area.
3. Follow the emergency procedures as listed above.

Small Fires:

1. Sound the fire alarm and immediately call 911—or other in your community.
2. Consider extinguishing the fire only if you are trained and properly equipped and if, in your judgment, you can do so safely.

Before Fighting a Fire, Make Sure You Have an Escape Route:

1. If fire cannot be extinguished using a portable fire extinguisher, or if the smoke presents a hazard, LEAVE THE AREA IMMEDIATELY.
2. Close the door to the area to confine and contain the fire.
3. Follow EMERGENCY PROCEDURES as listed above.
4. Follow all instructions given from the fire department and first responders.
5. Assemble outside the house of faith campus in designated areas.
6. Predesignated areas away from house of faith or campus.
7. Account for all individuals once assembled in designated areas.
8. Do NOT reenter the edifice or buildings on campus.
9. Reenter the buildings only after the all clear is given by the fire first responders.

Emergency Fire Procedure Guidance for House of Worship and Campus

What to Do if You Discover a Fire

1. If a fire occurs and smoke is detected or a burning odor.
2. Leave the area, closing all doors behind you. Do NOT LOCK.
3. Pull the closest fire alarm to initiate (BOTH) building evacuations.
4. Evacuate using the nearest exit.
5. Leave all items behind (e.g., purses or coats).

Telephone or Call the Fire Department Number in Your Area

In the United States, call 911 and report the following:

1. The location of the fire

2. The building's address
3. The suspected cause and status of the fire
4. Your name and cell phone or reachable number

Upon Hearing the Alarm or Announcement

1. Before opening the door, feel door bottom to top and knob with back of hand for heat.
2. If not hot, brace yourself against door and open slightly.
3. If you feel air pressure or hot draft, close door quickly.
4. If you find no fire or smoke in corridor, take your key, close door behind you, and leave by nearest exit.
5. If you encounter smoke in corridor or stairwell, consider taking corridor where another exit may be clear, or return to your room.

If Circumstances Prevent You from Leaving the Area

1. Close, but DO NOT LOCK THE DOOR for possible entry of firefighters.
2. Telephone the local fire department first responders and give name, building name and address, room number, floor number, and calmly explain the situation.
3. Wave sheet of paper in the window to alert firefighters.
4. Seal all cracks where smoke can get through.
5. Seal or shut off air-conditioning outlets if possible.
6. Stay low to the floor.
7. A roll of wide strong masking tape is useful.
8. Place wet towels under the door.
9. Crouch and crawl low on the floor if smoke enters the room and move to the most protected area.
10. Wait to be rescued. Remain calm. Do not panic.
11. LISTEN for instructions or information, which may be given by authorized personnel over loudspeakers.

Fire Drill Guidance

1. The purpose of a fire drill is to ensure that the house of worship staff and occupants are familiar with emergency evacuation procedures. This will result in orderly evacuation with efficient use of exit facilities.
2. Drills will be held annually at the worship house for the staff and congregation at predesignated times.
3. Drills will be *announced in advance* by social media, bulletins, word of mouth during service announcements, posting notices, and advising staff and other building occupants of the date and time.

*Specific fire training, drills, and evacuation instructions will be detailed in handouts for staff beforehand. Congregants will receive instruction at the discretion of clergy and senior leadership.

Staff Training and Drills Guidance

1. Conduct fire drills annually with the house of worship and the local fire and first responders.
2. The designated staff will attend a debriefing session to report on the actions and reactions of the participants and discuss any noted deficiencies.
3. All employees and regular building occupants will be instructed (trained) in fire safety precautions and emergency procedures.
4. Department heads of all programs and other designated staff will be instructed in their specific functions relating to fire safety.
5. Relevant sections of the fire safety plan will be reviewed biannually or annually with all the staff during regular meetings.
6. All new staff will receive orientation regarding the fire safety plan.

7. Clergy, teachers, stewards, ministerial staff, and trustees should review and explain the location of exits in bulletins, at conferences, and during new members' orientation.
8. Designated worship house staff will be trained in the use of fire extinguishers.
9. All staff will participate in a fire drill biannually or annually. Relevant sections of this fire safety plan will identify opportunities for improvement and update the current fire and evacuation plan.

After the emergency drill is completed, there may be specific issues to evaluate and discuss.

1. Transmission of alarm system.
2. Preparation and carrying out of proper procedures for building evacuation.
3. Assembly and accounting of all individuals (i.e., vulnerable populations, appropriate wheelchair protocols, and assembly to appropriate designated areas).
4. Overall following of written fire evacuation plan.
5. Fire extinguishers use RACE training.
6. Overall, how did the plan work?
7. What took us by surprise, and how do we mitigate lessons learned or avoid future mistakes?
8. What conditions were we unable to simulate so that everyone is prepared during a real or another fire emergency?
9. What hazards were around, and how do we remedy them?
10. What would be the next step going forward if this were a real disaster or emergency?
11. What changes should be made in our plan and coordination for the next drill?
12. How are you feeling?

Records and Storage Protocol

1. Records of all fire drills will be retained indefinitely as hard copies and use of hardware storage or other backup devices.

Preplanning Fire Drills with the Fire Department or Other First Responders

1. The local fire department and captain will be notified prior to holding a fire drill in case a house of worship staff calls them in the belief that there is a real fire.
2. The fire department will be called one hour before the drill or as specified by the leadership at the local fire department.
3. The caller will say, "This is a drill, this is a drill, this is a drill" (three times) and give the fire responders the exact location of where they are to report.
4. When the alarm sounds at the worship house and campus, all persons will be evacuated, following the prewritten evacuation plan.

Fire Safety Precautions

To avoid fire hazards in the building, occupants are advised to:

1. Keep stairwells, hallways, passageways, and exits always clear of obstructions and combustible refuse.
2. Always keep doors to stairways closed.
3. Ensure that electrically powered equipment—especially coffee makers, hot plates, and other kitchen appliances—are shut off when not in use, especially at the end of each business day.
4. Refrain from using unsafe electrical appliances, frayed extension cords, overloaded outlets, and lamp wire for permanent wiring.

5.   Do not use an appliance if you are unsure of its safety or you do not know how to use it.
6.   Keep heaters clear. Clothing, paper, and other articles should be kept away from heaters.

Alternate safety procedures during shutdown of fire protection equipment and systems between hours of operation:

1.   The house of worship will notify the local fire first responders and worship house occupants of any shutdown of fire protection equipment or systems. This will be done by the clergy or a designate.
2.   The alternate safety procedures during shutdown of fire protection equipment or systems will be posted in place of existing notifications.
3.   If the shutdown occurs during weekdays during day hours, staff will patrol the hallways once every hour or as often as feasible (but at intervals not to exceed three hours) during such shutdown. The designates will patrol the entire building and grounds during the fire drill and ensure that there are no conditions occurring that might constitute a fire hazard.

Maintenance Schedule for Fire Protection Protocol

Maintenance Definitions

1.   The fire protocol specifies requirements for checking, inspecting, and testing fire protection equipment and systems.
2.   Check means visual observation to ensure that a device or system is in place and is not obviously damaged or obstructed.

3. Inspect means physical examination to determine that the device or system will apparently perform in accordance with its intended function.
4. Test means operation of device or system to ensure that it will perform in accordance with its intended operation for function.

Record of All Tests Keeping Protocol

1. Records of all tests and corrective measures will be retained (saved) indefinitely as hard copies and use computer hardware storage or other backup devices.
2. Staff should back up computers regularly to preserve data in case of an emergency.
3. All fire system maintenance will be documented for each house of worship at every campus location.

Fire Department Access

1. Fire access routes shall always be maintained for immediate use by fire and first responders. The vehicle parking areas are always accessible and kept clear.
2. This is a local and state ordinance in most jurisdictions.

Emergency Exit Signs

1. Prevent vehicles from blocking the fire department and emergency vehicles in case of emergencies by enforcing towing in fire lanes and near fire hydrants.
2. Required exit signs shall be clearly visible and maintained in a clean and legible condition always.

Maintenance Schedule for Fire Protection Egress

(Means of Egress)
Maintenance Measures Frequency Conducted by Name and Title:

_____

Note: Report activity to clergy, trustee, or designee at regular meetings.

1. All exit doors should be easily open from indoors.
2. Exit doors should only lock from the outside.
3. Inspect doors in fire separations monthly.
4. Check doors in fire separations to ensure that they remain closed, as required by area laws and ordinance.
5. Maintain exit signs to ensure they are clear and legible as required.
6. Maintain exit lights to ensure they are illuminated and in good repair as required.
7. Maintain access to exits (e.g., corridors) and exits free of obstructions as required.

Emergency Lighting—Battery Pack Protocol

Maintenance Measures

1. Frequency check conducted by name and title:

   _____

2. Pilot lights checked for operation (to check if there is power to the unit) as required by manufacturer or laws.
3. Note: The emergency lighting system is tested annually by a certified contractor.

Maintenance Schedule for Fire Protection Systems and Equipment

(Fire Alarm System)
Maintenance Measures

1. Clergy and designated staff should know the location of main circuit breaker, main water valve, and other major building equipment.
2. All noted inspections are to be recorded in logbook or other computer storage locations.
3. Frequency check conducted by name and title:

_____

a) Regularly check fire alarm, AC power lamp, and trouble light.
b) Regularly check central alarm and control facility.
c) Regularly monitor for fire panel located in main entrance.
d) The following regular checks shall be conducted in accordance with the manufacturer's recommendations.
e) If a fault is established, appropriate corrective action shall be taken.

Example:

1. Visually check the principal trouble lights for trouble indication.

a) Green light: indicates the system is working
b) Yellow light: indicates the system is not working
c) Red light: indicates that THERE IS A FIRE

2. Check the AC power is lit to ensure its normal operation

    a) Note: the total system is checked monthly
    b) The system is tested annually by a certified contractor

3. Portable fire extinguishers.

    a) Maintenance measures examples:

- Frequency: conducted by persons as directed by Rabbi Cohen
- Regularly inspect all portable extinguishers as specified by manufacturers
- Maintain and test all portable extinguishers in conformance with NFPA

  - According to building codes in your specific location

- In the United States, National Fire Protection Association Annually:

  - This should be done by a hired company or follow local or state regulations.

CHAPTER 9

OCCUPATIONAL SAFETY AND HEALTH ADMINISTRATION (OSHA) GUIDANCE FOR FAITH HOUSES OF WORSHIP

The Occupational Safety and Health Administration (OSHA) Guidance

OSHA is part of the US Department of Labor and is headquartered in Washington, DC. The organization regulates private sector employers with more than one employee, including houses of worship.

OSHA distinguishes between the types of activities houses of worship perform but does not cover religious activities that houses of worship perform, such as religious worship or ministry services. However, secular activities that are covered include business office staff in administrative services, day care centers, bookstore employees, hospitals owned or operated by a religious organization, charitable organizations, private schools, or orphanages. They must comply with OSHA regulations as they contribute to and affect the economic sector of the United States society. OSHA regulations are in place to protect both the houses of worship and their congregations.

The focus is on employee's safety and training requirements. OSHA regulates the use of protective equipment and mitigates job accidents that may lead to employee injury or death.

Examples of *noncoverage* that pertain to religious organizations are clergy while participating or performing religious services—such as choir directors, organists, choir members, musicians, ushers, and the like.

All houses of worship are responsible to provide a safe working environment for its *employees, including contractors.*

OSHA Services

1. OSHA can inspect your house of worship at any time.
2. OSHA requires that employers have a written plan to facilitate escape in case of fire emergencies.
3. The training must emphasize employees be trained on what to do in an emergency.

4. Houses of worship clergy, leadership, or designees are required to inspect the house of worship campus, identify hazards, and make repairs to items that need fixing.

5. If a contractor hired to perform remodeling or any kind of work is injured, he or she may sue the contractor for violation of OSHA standards. The worship house can be sued as well—although they rely on the contractor's professional work.

6. Keep all *training records* in a safe location and assign administrative or designated staff to oversee its storage.

7. Any violations discovered during a site visit inspection can result in a fine for the house of worship. The fines can range from a few hundred to tens of thousands of dollars.

8. Your worship house is required by US laws to report any fatalities or injuries to OSHA and keep a log of all minor injuries.

9. The exact number of exits and fire extinguishers throughout the worship house depends on the size of the building(s). This includes chapels, meeting houses, and parishes on campus.

10. *All houses of worship should have health and safety training plans.*

11. There are services to assist your house of worship to become compliant.

12. OSHA offers education outreach and consulting services separate from the inspection division.

13. Numerous safety training firms are available at a low cost.

CHAPTER 10

HOSTAGE SITUATION PROTOCOL

Active Shooter Training—Shooter on Site by Hostile Intruder

(Additional information is available in the Mental Health section of this book)

Run, Hide, Fight

1. Look for and know where the nearest exits are within the house of worship and campus.
2. Have an escape plan in mind.
3. Run into (preidentified) or places you can hide.
4. Know and be prepared to evacuate or assist persons with disabilities anywhere on campus. The ushers and designees are responsible for assisting them to escape or hide.

What to Do in the Event of Crisis

Run and Escape, if Possible

1. Getting away from the shooter or shooters is the top priority.
2. Leave your purse and any belongings behind and get away.
3. If outdoors, proceed immediately to and inside meeting area or away from the shooter, and warn and prevent individuals from entering area where the active shooter may be.
4. If possible, evacuate and distance yourself, regardless of whether others agree to follow.
5. If indoors, help others to escape, if possible.

Hide if Escape Isn't Possible

1. Get out of the shooter's view and stay quiet.
2. Lock and block doors, close curtains and blinds, and turn off all lights.

3.   Do not hide in groups—spread out along walls or hide separately to make it more difficult for the shooter.

4.   Direct people to *drop*, *cover*, and *hold* until the situation is resolved.

5.   All congregants who are not responsible for people should take cover in the immediate area, if safe (this includes all campus facilities).

6.   Your hiding place should be out of the shooter's view.

7.   Remain calm, stay indoors until *all clear* signal is given, regardless of length of time.

8.   Silence initially, turn down (*off*) any cell phones, radios, or electronic devices that may bring attention to your whereabouts. Make sure they do not vibrate.

9.   Fight as an absolute last resort.

10. Commit to your actions and act as aggressively as possible against the shooter.

11. Recruit others to ambush the shooter with makeshift weapons—chairs, fire extinguishers, scissors, books, or whatever is available.

12. Be prepared to cause severe or lethal injury to the shooter.

13. Take care of yourself first, then help the wounded before first responders arrive, if possible.

14. If the injured in the congregation are in immediate danger, help get them to safety.

15. Call 911 when you are safe and describe shooter, location, and weapons. Try to communicate with the police silently. Use text message or social media to tag your location or put a sign in a window.

16. While you wait for first responders to arrive, provide first aid. Apply direct pressure to wounded areas and use tourniquets if you have been trained to do so.

17. Turn wounded people onto their sides if they are unconscious and keep them warm.

Afterward

When law enforcement officials arrive, follow this protocol:

1. When police or law enforcement arrives and gives you all clear, put your hands up high above your head before making a move to stand or leave. Keep hands visible and empty.
2. Know that law enforcement's first task is to end the incident, and they may have to pass injured along the way.
3. Officers may be armed with rifles, shotguns, or handguns and may use pepper spray or tear gas to control the situation.
4. Officers will shout commands and may push individuals to the ground for their safety.
5. Follow law enforcement instructions and evacuate in the direction they came from unless otherwise instructed.

Additional Guidance

1. Intruder in the building or active shooter clergy and key staff should establish a *code* word or words for intruder in the building and to address anyone threatening harm in the house of worship.
2. Consider post-traumatic stress disorder (PTSD) training or professional help for families or individuals within the congregation to cope with the long-term effects of the trauma.

Hostage Situation Protocol

Remain calm, evaluate the situation, take action.

1. Remain calm. Talk with intruder in a low, nonthreatening manner.
2. Do not make sudden movements.
3. Keep your distance.

4. Do not attempt to deceive or threaten the intruder.
5. Maintain order among the congregation and visitors.
6. Be consistently alert and prepared for violence.
7. In any hostage situation, the primary concern must be the safety of the congregation.

Note

a) Individuals who take hostages are frequently emotionally unstable.
b) Do not antagonize them.
c) Communication must be handled in a calm, quiet, non-threatening manner.
d) Remember, it may take little to cause such people to escalate to violence.

Bomb Threats

What to do if a bomb threat is received by phone:

1. If the threat of explosion is immediate, evacuate all people from the buildings and premises at once.
2. Follow the fire evacuation plan.
3. If the caller indicates there is some time before the bomb will go off:

   a) Try to get as much information as possible about the location and description of the bomb and the caller.
   b) Stay on the line only if the caller continues to provide useful information.
   c) Immediately evacuate the premises, taking the information provided with you.
   d) In the United States, call 911 first or the clergy or persons on the call-down list designated to handle

emergencies and convey all the information. (Call first responders in your area.)

What to Do If a Bomb or Explosive Device Is Discovered

1. Evacuate immediately.
2. Call police by dialing 911 out of building (fire department and hazmat team will respond).
3. Call postal inspectors if the item was received in the mail (877-876-2455) or protocols or number in your location.

Mailroom Security Guidance or Discovery of Suspicious Item

1. If you are unable to verify mail contents with the address or sender and there is no return address on the letter or package, if you find an item you suspect is a *bomb*, looks suspicious, or looks out of place, *do not touch, move, or disturb the item.*
2. What are the warning signs of a suspicious item?

   a) Discoloration or crystallization on the package
   b) Oily stains
   c) The presence of excessive tape or string
   d) If the package is rigid or bulky
   e) Strange odor
   f) If the package is lopsided or uneven
   g) Misspelled words
   h) If the letter is addressed to a title only:

      a. If the title is incorrect
      b. If the writing on the letter is badly typed or written
      c. If the item is possibly mailed from a foreign country

    d.   Call 911 or another designated church member or emergency number.

    e.   Notify the appropriate individual.

    f.   Keep persons away from the area until help (emergency responders) arrive.

The acronym SLAP is defined as:

S (Shape): Is there an unusual shape?
L (Look): Is there an unusual look?
A (Address): Is there an unusual look?
P (Package): Is there something unusual about the packaging?
US Postal Inspectors phone: 877-876-2455 or follow protocol in your area.

CHAPTER 11

WEATHER EMERGENCIES

What to Do before and during Weather Emergencies

Severe weather policy outline:

1. If you are outside, immediately seek shelter.
2. If you are inside, stay away from windows and glass doors.
3. Use stairwells, not elevators.

Hurricane Event Policy Outline

Tornado and High Wind Safety Guidance

1. The greatest threats from high winds caused by tornado, hurricane, thunderstorm downbursts, or a strong pressure surge behind a cold front are:

    a) roof failure;
    b) falling trees or tree limbs;
    c) breaking glass; and
    d) flying debris (airborne missiles).

2. The most dangerous locations are large rooms with big expansive roofs. The collapse of the room's load-bearing wall can lead to the failure of the entire roof.
3. Rooms with large windows may shatter from being struck by airborne objects and are extremely dangerous.
4. Small interior rooms, bathrooms, and windowless interior hallways that are away from exterior doors offer the best protection. All doors should be and remain closed. The lower level of the building is usually the safest.
5. If a severe storm warning is issued, church school students and teachers should be moved from unsafe areas of classrooms into hallways or restrooms on the first floor or lower level.

6. If the congregation anywhere is under a hurricane warning, find safe shelter immediately.

7. Shelter in place or evacuate if told to do so.

8. Take refuge in a designated area (*interior room*) for high winds within the sanctuary or campus.

9. Designated staff and teachers should listen for emergency alerts, watch storms as they approach, and prepare to take special actions.

10. If there has been no warning and people are still in the classrooms when that freight train sound is heard or the sound of breaking glass or structure failure (whether from wind or a bomb), the safest thing to do is to drop beneath the desks and chairs and cover your head and neck areas with both hands.

11. Designated staff should know how to shut off the main power (electricity) and gas if needed for safety purposes.

12. Only use generators outdoors and away from windows.

13. Have needed supplies available for at least three days or more if your worship house is providing community shelter.

What to do if anyone is trapped in the sanctuary or campus building:

1. If trapped in a campus building due to flooding, go to the highest level of the building.

2. Avoid wading in floodwater, which can be dangerous due to debris or electrical lines.

3. Save phone calls for emergencies. Phone systems are often down or busy after a disaster. Use text messages or social media to communicate.

4. Document any facility damage with photographs.

Earthquake Event Policy Outline

During an Earthquake

1. If you are inside, cover your head and crouch under the table or in a corner away from windows and exterior walls.
2. If you are outside, seek area away from power lines, trees, and buildings.

After an Earthquake

1. Do not rush outside.
2. Never use an elevator until it has been inspected for safety.
3. Use stairwells only after advised that they are safe.
4. Do not use matches or lighters in case there is leaking natural gas.
5. Cell or smartphones are a valuable resource during and after earthquakes, battery backups (solar chargers) are suggested. However, cell towers may malfunction, and wireless networks may become congested.
6. Telephones (landlines) in buildings, while considered old-fashioned, should be used for emergency calls and may be the only way to reach someone in the event of an emergency.
7. It is typical for aftershocks to occur for several days following the initial quake.
8. Aftershocks usually become less severe with time.

Weather Advisories

1. Watches. Hurricane tropical storm watch: The National Weather Service (NWS) issues a storm warning within forty-eight hours.
2. Warnings. Hurricane tropical storm warning, tropical storm is expected within thirty-six hours.

3. Extreme wind warning: when there is an imminent threat of extreme wind associated with a major hurricane.

4. Evacuation notices: If the danger is significant, local authorities may issue an evacuation notice to alert residents to leave the area immediately.

   a) Listen to emergency reports and take appropriate action.
   b) Evacuate when instructed to avoid being trapped by rising water.
   c) If conditions remain unsafe, delay congregants' departure.
   d) When dismissed from the sanctuary, turn around, do not drown. Do not walk, swim, or drive through floodwaters.
   e) Never attempt to outrun a tornado or remain outdoors during a severe thunderstorm.

CHAPTER 12

EVACUATION TRAINING PLAN

Evacuation Training

Avoid a disorganized evacuation; it can result in confusion, injury, and property damage.

1. The clergy and his designee, evacuation team leaders, and assigned employees are responsible for making the decision to evacuate the premises. It is critical that the congregation know who has the authority to make decisions during any emergency.
2. Walk throughout the worship house campus and ensure exit signs have sufficient lighting so congregants and guest can safely walk to all exits.
3. Remember: exits should never be blocked.
4. Security staff, trustees, ushers, stewards, class, and ministerial staff all should be trained. Clergy may plan walk-throughs in which *the staff practices evacuation procedures before training is offered to the congregations* during annual, biannual, or impromptu drills.
5. Clergy, security, trustees, and other key designated staff are responsible for sounding distinctive alarms, alerting, and calling the fire department or the police—in the United States, 911 or protocols in your location.
6. Predetermine the order of evacuations throughout the campus.
7. Head count: ushers, trustees, stewards, teachers, or designees should be assigned to take a head count during every service, meeting, or all activities on the worship house campus. This practice ensures safety and awareness of people present in case of an emergency.
8. The clergy or designees will assess the situation to determine whether an emergency exists requiring activation of the emergency procedures—such as evacuation, shelter in place, and so on. These designees must be trained and

immediately capable of recognizing when to abandon the building and evacuate.

9. Keep people on each floor together to make head count easier.

10. Direct congregants to an alternate safe exit; if an exit is blocked, enter every stairwell, walk down the stairs, and open exit doors to the outside if possible.

11. Continue walking away from the campus to the predetermined safe assembly area.

12. No one should leave the assembly area until the all clear is given by first responders or leadership.

13. Church administration should have oversight and methods in place to know who is on site in case of emergency—in-and-out boards or other sign-in procedures are helpful.

14. Security staff, trustees, ushers, stewards, class leaders, and ministerial staff should assist in evacuating all persons during emergencies and coordinate crowd control. All participants should understand the location of main evacuation routes and alternate routes.

15. Countermeasures and responses are situation-specific. Rooms and offices that can be secured or locked from the inside where people can hide should be selected in advance if possible.

16. Ensure elevators are not used during an emergency evacuation.

17. Procedures for shutdown of critical operations or other essential building equipment (i.e., shutdown valves) should be in the training plan for specific designated staff.

18. In the event of an emergency, local emergency management officials may order the church to evacuate the premises. In some cases, they may instruct the designated staff to shut off water, gas, or electricity.

19. Make sure all vehicles used for transportation have cell-phones, money, and mapping capability.

20. Determine if persons in need of transportation have relatives who can pick them up from the assembly areas.

21. Be sure to notify local authorities and alternate receiving facilities if the evacuation is at another off-site location (i.e., emergency shelter or hospital).

Supplies and Go-Kits

1. Worship houses should have go-kits at specific locations on- and off-site. Each worship house should determine specific items such as: contact cards, insurance data, flashlights, batteries, cellphones, writing utensils, floor plans, or any important item and possible needed information that should be available on each campus or alternate location.

Rescue Duties Protocol for Special Needs and Vulnerable Populations

2. The signal to evacuate must be well understood by all. Use of tactile devices may be necessary to alert congregants who would not otherwise be able to recognize an audible or visual alarm due to language and visual barriers.

3. The special needs congregants or guests may need other accommodations, such as sign language interpreters if these volunteers are on-site.

4. Assign trained security, trustees, or ushers to assist the disabled members and guests who are wheelchair bound, senior citizens, visually impaired, non-English speaking, or having other disabilities or special needs during an emergency.

Accounting for Congregants
After an Evacuation

1. Inform emergency personnel if anyone is missing, left, or stuck in the building or stairwells.

2. Accounting for church members and ensuring everyone evacuated out of buildings is important.

3. Confusion in the assembly areas can lead to delays in rescuing anyone trapped in the worship house and other buildings on the campus. In addition, unnecessary search and rescue operations may occur.

4. The designated assembly areas should be a safe distance away from the campus.

5. Take a head count after the evacuation. Identify the names and last known locations of anyone not accounted for and pass the information to the person in charge.

6. Notify the police, the fire department, and designated staff if someone is missing during an emergency.

7. Train and admonish all people present *to not go anywhere except the designated meeting place after they are evacuated from the buildings on campus.*

8. You do not want emergency personnel risking their lives searching for anyone. Because they (we) will not know who got out safely or if anyone wanders off to go home or leave the group.

9. Do not leave the designated meeting place until you are debriefed and the *all clear is announced.*

10. Assigned trustees, ushers, and security teams will provide crowd control in the parking lots and designated meeting reunification sites.

11. Ideally, the meeting reunification site will be further away but within safe walking distance, especially for those persons with special needs—evacuation and lack of transportation can be challenging.

12. Security personnel or law enforcement personnel should be present to ensure the safety of the congregants.

Shelter In-Place or Long-Term In-Place Sheltering

1. Evacuating congregants and guests may not be the best response to an emergency such as a tornado, hurricane, windstorm, thunderstorm, hailstorm, public health emergency, or toxic gas release.

2. In-place sheltering may be short-term, such as remaining in a safe place for a fairly short period while a tornado warning is in effect or while a chemical cloud passes. We also use the term "shelter" for houses of worship or other mass care facilities that provide a place to stay, along with food and water to people who evacuate following a disaster. It may be necessary for leadership, congregants, and guests to create a barrier between themselves and outside toxins or dangers.

    a) Cover all doors and vents with 2–4 mil. thick plastic sheeting.
    b) Cut the plastic sheeting several inches wider than the opening and label each sheet (i.e., fan, vent, window).
    c) Duct tape plastic at corners first, then tape all edges.

3. The guidance for houses of worship is usually a supply of seventy-two-hour nonperishable food and water.

    a) Nuts and peanut butter are a food allergy alert.
    b) One (1) gallon of water for each person or store enough for emergencies.

4. Remain in the shelter until local authorities say it is *okay* to leave.

5. Maintain a twenty-four-hour communication and safety watch. Take turns listening for radio broadcast and monitor your tone-alert weather radio.

6. Instructions for assembling a basic sanitary facility toilet:

7. Use a garbage container, pail, or bucket with a snug-fitting cover. If the container is small, use a larger container with a cover for waste disposal. Line both containers with plastic bags. After each use, pour or sprinkle a small amount of disinfectant or bleach into the container to reduce odor and germs.

CHAPTER 13

MEDICAL EMERGENCY AND HEALTH CARE TRAINING

Medical Emergency and Health Care Protocol

Trained and certified staff are often responsible for handling medical emergencies.

1. Call 911 immediately and do a follow-up call to designated individuals listed on emergency contact or call-down lists.
2. Identify your location—building name on campus, street address, and floor or specific area.
3. Calmly describe the situation or emergency:

   a) What happened or is happening (e.g., heart attack or fainting spell)?
   b) Specific injury (e.g., fall on ice).
   c) Help or type of assistance needed (e.g., ambulance).

4. Provide on-site first aid if you are qualified.
5. Designated and certified staff should be aware of and know the location of the first-aid kit.
6. Designated staff should maintain the supplies within the first-aid kit.
7. The clergy or designees who are responsible for verifying persons with medical certification. Ensure these certified individuals are available or on duty.
8. Alert appropriate individuals who are responsible for any personnel or congregants preapproved or saved medical information and instructions on file (i.e., medical alert bracelet, diabetes, or cardiac history).
9. Designated individual should be chosen to notify family or legal guardian as appropriate and preapproved for all youth under legal age and special needs congregants.
10. Only trained and certified personnel at your worship house who are certified to administer first aid/CPR should administer medical assistance. (Note: issues of legal liability should be considered by clergy and leadership.)

11. Be sure someone on the security team is in the parking lot to direct the emergency responders.

Medical Emergency Advanced First Aid (Bleeding Control Kits)

Research shows that bystanders with the right tools—with little or no training—can save lives. Having congregants and medical staff trained in using the tools in a bleeding control kit can be the key to preventing tragedy or death in critical first minutes before help arrives. Bleeding to death can happen within minutes. Without proper life-saving equipment and action, a person can bleed out before first responders or help arrives.

What goes in a bleeding control kit?

1. Tourniquets. One of the most critical pieces of life-saving equipment the bleeding control kit can have. It stems arterial bleeding in a victim's extremities. Various designs are readily available; tourniquets that are approved by the armed forces of the United States for use in battlefield trauma care are highly recommended or use whatever is available.

2. Chest seals. Created specifically to treat a sucking chest wound. These chest wounds are often from a gunshot, stabbing, or puncturing, and make a new pathway for air to travel in and out of the chest, which can result in collapsed lungs.

3. Compression bandages. One of the best ways to stop traumatic bleeding. Compression bandages allow you to keep sustained pressure on a wound while freeing your hand to address other issues.

4. Bleeding control bandages. Deep wounds need to be packed with gauze to control the bleeding. When done correctly, it can significantly reduce the time that direct pressure must be applied to arterial wounds. Some bandages also

are treated with hemostatic agents that make these efforts
more effective.

5.   Space emergency blankets. Severe trauma can lead to shock
     and hypothermia. Shock happens when there is not enough
     blood circulating through the body to keep organs and tis-
     sue functioning normally. Hypothermia decreases a per-
     son's ability to form clots. Keeping the body warm delays
     the onset of shock and maintains the body's ability to clot.

6.   Latex-free gloves. In a situation that requires a bleeding
     control kit, there will likely be other bodily fluids too.
     Nitrile exam gloves offer the wearer and the patient some
     protection from infection and blood-borne illnesses such as
     HIV and hepatitis.

7.   Scissors. During a traumatic high-stress event, getting to a
     wound to treat it might mean removing clothing. It is often
     safer and quicker to cut away the clothing than to move the
     patient around.

8.   Markers. A marker can be used to write on a variety of sur-
     faces, including paper, tape, tourniquet flaps, compression
     bandages, and skin to record the time aid was rendered.
     This provides first responders crucial information needed
     to render the best care.

9.   Instruction documents. HB 496 specifically calls for instruc-
     tional documents developed by the American College of
     Surgeons or by the US Department of Homeland Security.
     They detail methods to prevent blood loss following a trau-
     matic event. The instructions help readers prioritize which
     injuries to treat first and how.

CHAPTER 14

MENTAL HEALTH INCIDENTS AND CRISIS MANAGEMENT

Potential Attack Indicators

Behavior Profile of Bad Actors

Persons who pose a threat and plan to carry out attacks might engage in various behaviors that raise concern. Law enforcement or others in the community may know the individual and have knowledge of a person's upbringing, personal history, or current situation including community conflicts. Occasionally, the individual is dealing with negative life events and having gone through mental health services, hospitalization, or judication with arrests history.

The perpetrators may be known or unknown to the congregation. Most of the time these individuals have no prior history of unlawful behavior (i.e., active shooters).

While there is no lack of compassion from the religious community, this person could pose a danger to themselves or others. Mental illness may be a contributing factor, but its impact on the perpetrator's behavior is speculative or conjecture.

The literature in law enforcement, secret service, the Department of Homeland Security, Houses of Worship Security Practices Guide, May 2013, and psychological profiles show that many active shooters were described as social isolates and harbored feelings of hate and anger with a history of reported contact with mental health professionals. Life events or triggers include loss of significant relationships, loss of job impacting financial status, other adverse changes in circumstances, feeling forgotten, looked down upon, rejected, powerless, and substance use or abuse as a cause of the psychological and social profiles.

Insanity Defense Reform Act of 1984

The act was signed into law by President Ronald Reagan on October 12, 1984, amending (revision) the United States federal laws governing defendants with mental diseases or defects to make it significantly more difficult to obtain a verdict of not guilty only by reason of insanity. It removed the volitional component (*individual will or decision they make*) that a defendant lacked capacity to conform their conduct to the law from the ALI test (ALI is a test established by the American Law Institute Model Penal Code, which provides that a defendant would not be criminally responsible for conduct). Defendants were exculpated (clear from alleged fault or guilt) only if "at the time of the commission of the acts constituting the offense, as the result of a severe mental disease or defect, [they were] unable to appreciate the nature and quality or wrongfulness of their acts." The law passed in the wake of public outrage after John Hinckley Jr.'s acquittal by reason of insanity for his attempted assassination of President Ronald Reagan.

Prior to the enactment of the law, the federal standard for insanity was that the government had to prove a defendant's sanity beyond a reasonable doubt (assuming the insanity defense was raised). Following the act's enactment, the defendant has the burden of proving insanity by "clear and convincing evidence." Furthermore, expert witnesses for either side are prohibited from testifying directly as to whether the defendant was legally sane or not but can only testify as to their mental health and capacities, with the question of sanity itself to be decided by the finder-of-fact at trial. The act was held to be constitutional (and the change in standards and burdens of proof are discussed) in *United States v Freeman*.

It was criticized by psychologist Lawrence Z. Freedman for being ineffective. "If the attacker is rational mentally, stable emotionally, and fanatic politically, he will not be deterred. Nor will an irrational, effectively disturbed individual be deterred."

In my clinical experience, some persons were sent to forensic psychiatric hospitals (a secure facility that treats and rehabilitates individuals who have come in conflict with the law. They are deemed unfit to stand trial or not criminally responsible due to mental illness. Individuals with other criminal pathology (i.e., sociopathic/antisocial behavior) are sent to jail where they receive psychiatric services while incarcerated.

Leading Up to the Attack Imminent Behavioral and Surveillance Indicators

There are of observable behaviors that may precede an attack—for example, the perpetrator may surveil a potential target or there may be evidence that your house of worship was being monitored. These suspicious individuals may be in the vicinity attempting to gather information, observing your operations, or the coming and going of staff schedules, working hours, volunteers, and congregants. All suspicious activity should be observed and reported by staff, volunteers, and congregants.

They may seek out and engage in training or beginning mobilization in advance of the attack. Beware of suspicious persons in crowded areas wearing unusual bulky clothing that might conceal guns or explosives, or unexpected or unfamiliar delivery trucks arriving at the facility, or unattended packages (i.e., backpacks, briefcases, boxes), including suspicious packages or letters in the mailroom. Recent damage to perimeter fence or gate or lighting on worship house campus.

Immediate action needs to be taken and requires an immediate response, so call 911 or local law enforcement in your area.

Mental Health Incidents and Crisis Management Protocol and Policy

Illness within the church-wide campus includes mental health issues, abhorrent or disruptive behavior.

In a volatile situation or critical incident, our primary responsibility is the safety of all congregants and guests. This guidance will assist you once repetitive disruptive behavior has occurred or actual threats have been made.

Domestic Violence and Restraining Orders

Members of the congregation should be asked to inform worship house leadership or staff designee, if they have placed a restraining order against anyone or if there are issues related to child custody, business conflicts, or similar situations that might erupt into violence at the place of worship. The congregant should be assured of confidentiality, except on a need-to-know basis.

VIOLENCE PREVENTION POLICY FOR HOUSES OF WORSHIP

This house of worship maintains the policy that any violent acts or threats of the same, made by anyone on campus property against another person's life, health, well-being, family, or property, are entirely unacceptable and cause for an immediate intervention or immediate dismissal by the following: security personnel, crisis management team, ushers, trustees, stewards, clergy, or senior management.

This policy holds for any threats made on worship house property, at any events, or in other circumstances that may negatively affect the worship house's ability to function (i.e., provide transportation on vans). Such acts or threats of violence, whether made directly or indirectly by words, gestures, or symbols, infringe upon our house of worship's right or obligation to provide a safe environment for all attendees and staff.

Anyone who believes that he or she has been the target of violence or has witnessed or otherwise learned of violent conduct by anyone on campus property in the capacity described above should contact any of the persons described above.

The above policy will serve to assist all congregants and guests and reduce or mitigate potential liability by educating senior leadership.

Basic Rules for Violence Prevention

1. Treat everyone with respect.
2. Welcome all congregants and guests.
3. Try to spot trouble before it starts. We can often spot trouble and head it off by staying alert and in control of ourselves.
4. Trust your feelings. Our instincts—feelings of dread, uneasiness, spiritual discernment, and so on—are important warning signs. Heed them!
5. Always follow proper violence prevention procedures and *take all threats seriously.*
6. Report every incident. All threats and potential sources of trouble should be reported.
7. Do not try to be a hero. Stay calm and always think before you act.

Tips on Nonverbal Communication

1. Pay attention to the nonverbal communication that you express toward the threat maker or violent individual and that he or she exhibits toward you.
2. Communication experts point out that 10 to 15 percent of the messages we deliver to another person is the verbal element and 85 to 90 percent of the message is nonverbal.
3. Give the potentially violent person enough physical space. Although this may vary by culture, in the United States, two to four feet away is considered an adequate and safe distance.
4. Do not turn your back and be ready to escape quickly if necessary.
5. Avoid glaring or staring, which may be perceived as a challenge.
6. Stay conscious of how you are delivering your words. Keep the volume low and speak calmly.

7. Listen carefully. Use empathetic listening without judgment. Use silence as a calming tool, paraphrase to clarify what you are hearing. Acknowledge the person's feelings and ask questions. Do not accept blame for the problem.
8. Offer the person choices, giving him or her a way out of the situation. Suggest ways the problem can be resolved.
9. Observe the individual's body language. Use caution if the person exhibits one or more of the following:

• red face	clenched jaws
• sweating	exaggerated gestures
• pacing	shallow, rapid breathing
• trembling or shaking	scowling or sneering
• crossed arms and legs	glaring or avoiding eye contact

Remain calm and as nonthreatening as possible.

Managing Crisis Situations

If reunification is not possible because congregants are missing, injured, or killed, family members need to be notified as soon as possible. The planning team who will be responsible for this critical task should be selected within the house of worship beforehand.

While law enforcement is trained to take the lead on death notifications and injury protocols, all select staff should be trained in their role and responsibilities before the occurrence of critical incidents. Law enforcement and medical examiner procedures should be followed. Family members and next of kin or legally responsible caretakers should receive accurate and timely information with compassion.

The house of worship's emergency operations safety plan should include both written resources and local points of contact to work with and provide support to family member and caretakers.

This should include federal victim assistance personnel, clergy, counselors internal and external, police officers, and other first responders within your community. These points of contact are recommended by state and federal emergency agencies and should be connected to families early during the emergency—including while the individual is still missing or if any victims have been positively identified.

It is important that family members and caretakers receive long- and short-term support services. This include strategies for families who choose not to be engaged in interacting with the media either before or after the emergency or incident.

Caregiver Emergency Contact Information

Contact information for all congregants should be kept up to date. This information is critical to the reunification process for parents, children, legal guardians, and caretakers. Hard copies of this information could be kept in paper files, cards, and binders for quick access and portability. During an emergency event (evacuation), keep in mind electronic information may not be available. This could be due to power outages, lack of available computers or cell phones. These cards should be kept alphabetically for quick access. In church and worship house schools, this information could be organized by grade level with family contact information and caregivers who are authorized to pick up the students. Also list those persons with custodial and contact restrictions to ensure children are released to legal guardians and authorized caregivers.

Mental Health Counseling Before, During, and After the Incident

Post-Traumatic Stress Disorder Overview

Post-traumatic stress disorder (PTSD) is a debilitating psychological condition triggered by a major traumatic event such as a terrorist act, a shooter incident, the death of a loved one, a public health emergency, a natural disaster, or any catastrophic event.

It is marked by upsetting memories or thoughts of the ordeal, blunting of emotions, increased arousal, and sometimes severe personality changes.

Officially termed "post-traumatic stress disorder" since 1980, PTSD was once known as shell shock or battle fatigue. This was due to more common manifestation by war veterans. However, in the past twenty or more years, PTSD has been diagnosed in rape victims and those subjected to violent crime. Examples are survivors of the September 11, 2001, World Trade Center and Pentagon terrorist attacks, as well as school and workplace shootings.

Adults and children are susceptible to PTSD. Children may experience learning disabilities and memory or attention problems. They may become anxious, dependent, or self-abusing.

First-response emergency personnel and individuals directly involved or children and families who have lost loved ones are more likely to experience PTSD.

Amid the COVID-19 outbreak, PTSD rates among medical professionals treating patients on the front lines put them at risk for depression and suicide.

Symptoms usually begin within three months of the trauma although sometimes PTSD does not develop until years after the trauma has occurred. Once the symptoms begin, they may fade away within six months. Others suffer with the symptoms far longer and the condition may become chronic.

Among the most troubling symptoms are flashbacks, which can be triggered by images, smells, sounds, or feelings. During a flashback, the person relives the trauma and may completely lose touch with reality. They may suffer for minutes or hours, believing that the trauma is happening all over again. It is possible to have a mild PTSD reaction following less severe stress.

Trained Personnel and Mental Health Support Services

A mental health professional should diagnose the condition. The house of worship should identify medical and mental health emergency intervention teams beforehand to be included in the plan. These crisis response teams (CRT) should be included in your list with other first responders and community partners.

Post-Traumatic Stress Disorder Counseling for Volunteers and Clergy Designees

During a mass casualty, clergy, staff, counselors, nurses, designees, and volunteers should use available counseling. They should monitor and support one another. They are encouraged to monitor one another's stress level and performance. Frequent breaks should be encouraged and discuss feelings with others on the support team. In addition, they should stay hydrated and eat healthy. Twelve-hour shifts are recommended.

Encourage counseling during deactivation or when the crisis event has ended.

Healing the Healers

International Critical Incident Stress Management Organization (ICISF.org)

Critical Incident Stress Management (CISM) Overview

Critical incident stress management (CISM) is a method of helping first responders and others who have been involved in critical incidents that leave them emotionally and/or physically affected by those incidents. CISM is a process that enables peers to help their peers understand problems that might occur after an event. This process also helps people prepare to continue to perform their services or, in some cases, return to a normal lifestyle. Its purpose is to enable people to return to their daily routine quickly and with less likelihood of experiencing PTSD.

ICISF provides training for individuals interested in becoming a part of a crisis management team or for an organization that is dedicated to helping individuals or groups recover from incidents.

CISM is an adaptive, short-term psychological helping process that focuses on an immediate and identifiable problem. It can include pre-incident preparedness to acute crisis management and post-crisis follow-up. The intervention works best for small groups of eight to twelve people.

Some researchers conclude CISM is ineffective for primary trauma victims and should only be used for secondary victims, such as responding emergency services personnel.

CISM allows the volunteers or first responders to discuss their feelings about the incident, when it happens, without judgment or criticism. The program is peer driven and the people conducting the interventions may come from all walks of life. However, most are first responders—police, fire, emergency medical services personnel, or work in the mental health field—and all intervention meetings are strictly confidential. These changes should be reported if the person who receives assistance is determined by the interventionist to be a danger to themselves or others. The emphasis is keeping people safe and returning them to their levels of functioning.

The purpose of the intervention process is to establish stress levels as normal as possible. Critical incidents are traumatic and cause powerful emotional reactions to people who are exposed to them. The most stressful are line-of-duty deaths, coworker suicide, multiple event incidents, delayed intervention, and public health and multi-casualty incidents. Others include serious injury, disaster terrorism incidents, rape, significant events involving children, and any powerful overwhelming distressing event.

The Goal of the Intervention

The trauma is addressed along four general progressions:

1. Defusing. Done the day of the incident before the persons has a chance to sleep. It is usually conducted within twelve hours of a critical incident. Its purpose is to validate people's feelings, inform them of what symptoms to watch for over the short-term, and offer them a lifeline or telephone number where they can talk with someone. Defusings are limited to individuals directly involved in the incidents and are informal, sometimes at the scene, and designed as coping mechanisms in the short-term to address immediate physical needs.
2. Debriefing. Usually the second level of intervention for those persons directly affected by the incident and often the first for those not directly involved. It is designed to assist in mitigating the long-term impact of the incident. A debriefing is normally done within seventy-two hours of the incident. It gives the individual or group the opportunity to talk about their experience and how it has affected them, brainstorm coping skills, identify individuals at risk, and inform the individual or group of services available to them in their community.
3. Follow-up. Final step is to follow up with them the day after the debriefing to ensure that they are safe and coping well or to refer the individual to professional counseling.
4. Additional follow-up. Final step, generally done within the week following the debriefing by team members as a check-in.

CISM Planning

CISM is recommended for congregant volunteers, lay leaders, ministers, and personnel. The clergy may choose to put in place advanced preparation for a crisis. Often the acute stress proves too difficult for the worship house teams of volunteers. This preplanning may provide the coping skills necessary during and after the critical event.

It is necessary to identify workers who may need professional mental health care. Ongoing support is available for individuals in need of coping skills and support.

> If the crisis event is beyond the capability of the house of worship, critical incident stress management is highly recommended.

Chapter 15

Firearms in Worship Houses

The Need or Use of Firearms in Worship Houses

A Brief Historical Overview

On December 20, 2012, in Toledo, Ohio, a man pleaded guilty to three counts of arson. He was charged one count each of intentionally defacing, damaging, and destroying religious property, using a fire to commit a felony, and using and carrying a firearm to commit a crime of violence. He was ordered to serve twenty years in prison and pay restitution to the mosque. This injustice occurred at the Islamic Center of Greater Toledo in Perrysburg.

On March 15, 2019, a self-confessed White supremacist was accused of killing fifty-one people in two New Zealand mosques. He was accused of opening fire in the Al-Noor and Linwood mosques in the worst mass shooting in New Zealand's recent history.

In March 2020, a judge ruled the terrorist will spend the rest of his life in prison. It is the first time under current New Zealand law that a sentence of life without the possibility of parole has been imposed.

On June 17, 2015, the Emanuel African Methodist Episcopal Church in Charleston, South Carolina, one of the oldest Black churches in the United States, has been often a center for civil rights. One day, they welcomed a young Caucasian man during the weekly Bible study. He worshipped with the group one hour before he shot and killed nine African Americans. Only three victims survived. He used a Glock 41 .45-caliber handgun—he had been carrying eight magazines holding hollow-point bullets. The shooter fled the scene of the mass shooting.

On October 27, 2018, the Tree of Life Jewish Synagogue in Pittsburgh, Pennsylvania, was the target of a mass shooting in which congregants were killed and seven injured. It was the deadliest attack on the Jewish community in the United States. A gunman armed with an AR-15 assault rifle opened fire inside of the synagogue. Just ahead of the shooting, the gunmen posted a racist comment about the invasion of immigrants. The clergy decided to hire an armed guard.

On July 25, 2019, an apparent hate crime occurred at a house on the property of the Hughson Sikh Temple, where an intruder at the Sikh Temple Modesto Ceres, California, broke windows at a priest's home on temple grounds, punched the priest, shouted obscenities, and told him to go back to his own country before fleeing, according to the priest and others associated with temple. The priest said he was in his bedroom about 9:30 p.m. when the glass in two-bedroom windows was broken. He said he lifted the blinds of one of the windows to look out and was punched in the neck before his attacker, who he said was wearing a mask, fled. The perpetrator said, "Country, country, country, go back, go back, country." Then the attacker proceeded to yell obscenities at him and had something in his hand to break the windows. Singh assumes the intruder ran off in the temple's nearby overflow, dirt parking lot.

House of Worship Security and Armed Security Guards

Professional Security Roles and Responsibilities

These individuals serve as representatives of the worship house and clergy. They are responsible for the overall safety and security of the congregation. The security guard's role is to make themselves clearly visible, as this will deter criminals. Most criminals think twice if they see a security guard on duty. They identify actions or situations that require quick action and response to control a myriad of emergency situations. How a security guard responds to any crisis varies depending on the threat.

Violence Response Planning

This security team provides a swift response to threats against active shooters. Your worship house should decide the necessity of armed paid or volunteer security guards. Each worship house must determine whether this armed team makes sense for them. Your situation, environment, and community determine your needed response capability and training practices. Should an unfortunate event occur, your congregation can hire or select current or former retired law enforcement professionals or security firms. One of the criteria for selection is security firms who receive weapons training and are certified, licensed, bonded, and insured. You are providing security experts who are visible to the congregation and any potential bad actors. No one is immune to being targeted.

Worship House Security Volunteers

Another consideration is the use of volunteers whose primary roles should be maintaining security within the house of worship. They could be supervised by a primary (head) security professional who would develop procedures with clergy for input and supervision. The staff may be off duty police officers, security personnel, and emergency medical services (EMS) fire personnel. They can be military retirees or personnel who are members of the worship house congregation with medical and emergency management background. They would be deployed during services or special events. The volunteers should wear clothing that identifies them as security (i.e., black jackets with security printed in bright colors on the front and back of the jacket). The lettering should be large enough to be seen at a reasonable distance. Portable radios (walkie-talkies) are recommended so they can communicate with one another from anywhere on the campus grounds. Security teams could be equipped with personal alarms or have access to panic buttons that send an alarm to police, fire, or EMS.

Armed Congregants Considerations

Open carry: a loaded or unloaded pistol carried upon an individual in which the pistol, holster, scabbard, or case is wholly or partially visible.

Note: a scabbard is a protective case for a gun or other weapon or tool.

The sight of a firearm might be emotionally difficult for many in the congregation as it does not or may not give the appearance of a welcoming and friendly house of worship. In this instance, professional security may work best for your congregants.

Concealed carry: a loaded or unloaded pistol and holster case hidden from the view and detection of others.

Legislation in some communities allows licensed and trained individuals with background checks to carry concealed handguns. They are legally permitted if trained in the use of deadly force, in defense of home, property, self, or others. A common-sense consideration is any armed individual who responds to a chaotic or an intruder, such as an active shooter in a crowded worship house, where multiple people may also choose to respond should consider personal liability.

Legal Liability Issues

Your liability should be considered, and your attorney's input can be helpful in assessing the risk related to your environment, zip code, zone, state, or region. In many issues related to tornado or earthquake, if someone is killed, harmed, become ill, or a child is abducted within the congregation, this may develop into a legal liability issue. In addition, houses of worship have become susceptible to lawsuits and claims for false accusations or inappropriate behavior. If someone claims any harm even if it is considered "acts of God," you should have at least general liability insurance coverage to protect the congregation.

If your security team (armed guards) uses excessive force, this may become a legal liability issue for the worship house.

CHAPTER 16

TIME MANAGEMENT AND PROCESS MAPPING

Why Process Mapping Is Important

A process map is a handy tool used by many organizations, like emergency management agencies and planners, to gain a better understanding of your process. It is especially useful when there are complicated plans to examine and write. In this case, the map is an outline or picture of everything that you anticipate happening within your planning process. It is often easier to begin at a top level of hierarchy and work your way down to the lower levels of detail. If you are already familiar with your planning process, you may choose to start at a lower level. As a suggestion, there should be no more than ten tasks at any one level. Simplify your process.

Time Frame Process Mapping (Sample)

1. April 12, 2019. Meeting to finalize and prioritize training needs and develop training opportunities to share with the ministry leadership, clergy, officers, stewards, trustees, ministerial staff, and congregation.
2. The final draft of the emergency preparedness plan with roles, duties, positions, and responsibilities will be completed for review by April 2019, as requested by leadership.
3. The approved copy will be edited as a brochure titled "The Disaster Preparedness Guide for the Houses of Worship." This brochure will serve as a model on how to condense and simplify all key points for house of worship clergy and ministerial leaders. Our Emergency Operations Plan (EOP) and grant application, once written and submitted by and for our worship house, will be streamlined for its components to be readily accessible for future training, exercises, and grant proposals.
4. Upon completion of the Emergency Operation Plan (EOP), I will request assistance from the trainers who have volunteered their time.
5. The plan is to train leadership first and then congregation.

6. Lauren Holley-Allen will submit the (EOP) to the house of worship clergy and other leadership as they had requested. Their deadline request was the end of April 2019 for final review.

7. Afterward, the final draft of the document will be forwarded to professional editors at Lauren Holley-Allen's expense.

8. The final copy of the Emergency Operation Plan (EOP) was given to the clergy and all board members in August 2019.

Prioritized instructor lead training is recommended for this house of worship by Lauren Holley-Allen with volunteers and local law enforcement partners.

1. First aid and cardiopulmonary resuscitation (CPR) courses (American Red Cross) partners.

2. Defibrillator training to include the exact location and maintenance (ARC).

3. Active shooter training for the entire congregation to include trainers, local police district partners, emergency teams, security committee with health ministry members or alternate.

4. Facility evacuation training and drill in the event of fire, bomb, or any emergency.

   a) Evacuations of all from campus-related programs.
   b) Evacuation of all guests and visitors always.
   c) Shelter-in-place plan if circumstances prevent us from leaving the buildings or campus.
   d) Having an active shooter plan based on disciplined response.
   e) Fire safety training and drills to include fire and law enforcement partners.

CHAPTER 17

DRILLS AND EXERCISES

This section will describe the training objectives and exercise activities the worship house will use in support of the training and security plan. You will decide your drill frequencies based on the needs of your house of worship. What is important is that stakeholders understand their roles, responsibilities, and what is expected of them during an emergency event.

Content should also be based on country of origin, county, state, local government laws or ordinances, and it should include administrative requirements of the faith house and scheduling with local emergency management agency officials.

Exercises may range from basic fire and shelter in place to tabletop or full-scale community wide drills.

*All meetings should be mandatory and scheduled annually, biannually, monthly, or weekly unless stated otherwise.

Training Guidelines for Drills and Exercises

Periodic Tabletop Exercises and Drills
(Exercise the Emergency Safety and Security Plan)

The more the plan is practiced and the more congregants are trained, the more likely they will be able to act before, during, and after any incident. This will lessen the impact on life and property. Exercises are more effective if they provide opportunities to practice with local emergency officials and community partners. The drills will help you to recognize gaps in the existing plan and make needed changes as a team consensus.

Houses of worship conduct exercises and drills with the emergency team, security committee, and house of worship administrators as an organization to increase safety readiness. Drills will serve to teach our house of worship actions or protocols they need to perform during emergencies. The training allows the emergency teams with senior leadership to test and evaluate emergency plan effectiveness. It is important for everyone involved to understand the actions he or

she may be asked to take for their safety. The more individuals prepare, the safer your congregants will be during any emergency event.

As stated in previous chapters, walk-throughs in which the staff
practices evacuation themselves are highly recommended. It may be
impractical to have realistic drills when the full congregation is present and difficult to have regular drills with some volunteers as staff
turnover may be an issue.

Examples are discussions of the potential impact of weather-related events, concerning early dismissal and closing the edifice or
temple.

Discussions or information from or with the National Weather
Service (NWS) to determine the timeline and severity of an approaching storm is helpful if not mandatory.

If your faith house leadership choose to conduct drills, these
suggestions will clarify the benefits.

There are *three types* of *emergency preparedness drills* and two are
recommended for houses of worship.

1. Full-scale exercise preparedness drill
    (Not recommended, but leadership can attend out-
    side training for the experience.)
    A full-scale exercise is a multidiscipline, multi-juris-
    dictional exercise involving functional joint field office,
    emergency operations centers, public information centers,
    hospital staff, and bloody actors usually by the local emer-
    gency management agency and the Incident Command
    System (ICS) is in full activation.
    A full-scale drill is as close to the real thing as possible.
    It is a comparatively lengthy event and it is staged on loca-
    tion using as much equipment as possible, and personnel
    that would be called upon in a real event.
    Example: area hospitals are alerted for a surge of
    injured people.

2. Tabletop drill

    (Recommended for church leadership and trustees.)

    This is a facilitated analysis of an emergency in an informal, stress-free environment designed to elicit constructive *small group discussions*. Participants examine and resolve problems based on existing operational plans and identify where those plans need to be refined.

    The success of this drill is largely determined by group participation in the identification of problem areas and should include risk assessment worksheets. There is minimal attempt at simulation in a tabletop exercise and the participants verbally assess or walk through scenarios and the courses of actions the house of worship will need before, during, and after an incident. Equipment is not used, resources are not employed, and time pressures are not introduced. This is a simple type of exercise to conduct in terms of planning, preparation, and coordination.

During drills, local emergency management officials and community partners may choose to perform a walk-through of the actual grounds, buildings, or campus to practice responding to emergency scenarios.

The risk assessment worksheet will assist our identification of potential hazards and threats.

This worksheet is a requirement of:

FEMA's *Guide for Developing High-Quality Emergency Operations Plans for Houses of Worship, June 2013.*

An emergency is an unforeseen situation that threatens the well-being and safety of our houses of worship and congregants. Emergencies may be natural or man-made, public health emergencies, and include floods, hurricanes, tornadoes, fires, toxic gas releases, chemical spills, explosions, civil disturbances, and active shooter or other violence resulting in bodily harm and trauma, or a flu epidemic or evolving pandemic.

The risk assessment was my initial recollection of "what if." The guidance is for the house of worship leadership to discuss, select, add the emergencies that might happen, and *document them on the chart.*

Example: Our house of worship scenario:

➢ We will brainstorm the worst-case scenarios and include them to our Emergency Operation Plan (EOP).
➢ Your commitment and support are critical to the plan's success.
➢ This task should be completed during our next meeting with or leadership.
➢ Attendance is mandatory.

---

3. Functional drill

(Recommended for congregation's evacuation and fire plan.)

This type of drill simulates an emergency in the most realistic manner possible, short of moving real people and equipment to an actual site. As the name suggests, its goal is to test or evaluate the capability of one or more functions in the context of an emergency event. Participants react to realistic simulated events, such as an intruder with a gun or a bomb threat. This drill is less expensive and involves multiple partners. The ICS procedures are used.

The framework we will utilize is the Incident Command System (ICS), a standardized approach to the command, control, and coordination of emergency response providing a common hierarchy within which our church responder personnel can be effective in accordance with our skill levels and secular work experiences.

ICS Defined

ICS consists of a FEMA-inspired standard management hierarchy and procedures for managing temporary incidents of any size.

CONCLUSION

Knowing and anticipating what to do when faced with an emergency or crisis *beforehand* can make the difference between life and death. The crisis is the time to follow the emergency operations plan in which staff have received training and exercises. This is not the time to make your plan from scratch. As indicated, training and exercises are of paramount importance to train your team's muscle memory before, if, or when an unfortunate crisis or attack occurs. Their effective response will minimize injury and potential loss of life.

Congregants may not know what to do during a crisis event and simply freeze or run in all directions. This is a normal human response, especially if people are not trained. House of worship readiness requires the total involvement of leadership at every level of planning.

This instructional guide is designed to prepare your staff, congregants, volunteers, and visitors to respond effectively during various crisis. You will be better prepared if you create your emergency safety and security plan before the crisis happens. You may operate for years without experiencing incidents, accidents, or tragedies that impact your house of worship.

A written and established emergency plan is your first level of defense for any man-made or natural disaster. Your secondary level of defense is a well-trained and drilled congregation. In addition, the relationships you have preestablished with your emergency management and other congregations in the community will provide needed assistance. When the crisis proves too difficult for your local city, county area police, or fire representatives, you can depend upon high levels of assistance and coordination with first responder teams, both state and federal—local emergency management agencies, Federal Emergency Management Agency (FEMA), the Federal Bureau of Investigation (FBI), the Army National Guard, the Public Health Department, and the Centers for Disease Control and Prevention (CDC). Nonprofit and private sector organizations are in place to provide assistance—American Red Cross and others.

This book addresses general preparedness, response training protocols to specific types of emergencies, and security resources. Mental health protocols are included that addresses worship houses pre- and post-concerns after a critical incident or other stressful events.

USEFUL FORMS

Record Keeping and Training

Every worship house will secure emergency plans and general policies and procedures differently.

All copies of training and exercises (drills) should be stored in the facility's secure networks of choice, including secure on- and off-campus locations for each house of worship.

The list includes sign-in sheets for each module, evaluations, drills and training assessment data, risk assessment records, continuity of operations plans, business impact analysis, instructional outlines, emergency contact listings, and more.

The following forms will be helpful and at your fingertips.

PRESENTATION AND PLANNING OUTLINE
Name of curriculum writer:
Date curriculum was written (submission date):
Course length or timing (length of time for the instruction: one-hour presentation):
Location: house of worship

PRESENTATION DEVELOPMENT
Topic or purpose of the presentation (purpose of this training is to ensure that you are aware of _____):
Goal:
The goal of this class (e.g., goal of this class is to provide a forum to increase understanding of or discuss and assess _____):
At the end of this presentation, the participant will understand the fire safety protocol for house of worship.
Objectives (these identify what the participant will achieve: at the conclusion of this training the participant will be able to _____):

- Define
- Discuss
- Identify
- Change

Example: Demonstrate the use of a defibrillator.
Teaching tools: audio/visual aids, including handouts to assist with the instruction
Examples of resources needed:

- ✓ PowerPoint deck
- ✓ Presentation materials
- ✓ Computer and projector
- ✓ Student handouts or booklets

Suggested Readings

Resources to read, review, and consider to enhance your understanding of evacuation protocols or instructed material.

This plan will be reviewed and updated biannually or annually by the emergency preparedness planning team members, as confirmed by their respective signatures and dates:

_____

Rabbi David Cohen, Chief Preparedness Officer

_____

Aadavan Acharya, Vice Chair

_____

Chair Pro-Tem of the Trustee Board, James Day

_____

Imam Abdul Dahman, Active Shooter Consultant

_____

Akaljot Amrit, Coordinator of Church Security

_____

Lauren Holley-Allen, MA, PSA, Author

_____

Father Richard Davis, Editor and Advisor to the Board
Date: _____

IN CASE OF FIRE: EMERGENCY CALL-DOWN LIST:

Clergy or Trustees:

Cell:

Home:

Designee: _____

Cell:

Home:

Designee: _____

Cell:

Home:

Risk Assessment Worksheet (Identified Threats and Hazards)

Hazards	Risk Possibility (Rate 1–10) 10 highest	Congregant/ Employee Impact	Property Impact	Economic Impact	Total Possible Impact
Active Shooter Event					
Hostage Situation					
Weather Events: Hurricane, Tornado, Winter Storm					
Bomb Threat/ Suspicious Items					
Medical Emergency					
Fire Safety					

Risk Assessment Worksheet (Identified Threats and Hazards and Risk Assessment)

Hazard	Probability	Magnitude	Warning	Duration	Risk Priority
Active Shooter Event	4. Highly Likely 3. Likely 2. Possible 1. Likely	4. Catastrophic 3. Critical 2. Limited 1. Negligible	4. Minimal 3. 6–1 hour 2. 12–24 hours 1. < 24 hours	4. 12+ hours 3. 6–12 hours 2. 3–6 hours 1. < 3 hours	High Medium Low
Hostage Situation	4. Highly Likely 3. Likely 2. Possible 1. Likely	4. Catastrophic 3. Critical 2. Limited 1. Negligible	4. Minimal 3. 6–1 hour 2. 12–24 hours 1. < 24 hours	4.12+ hours 3. 6–12 hours 2. 3–6 hours 1. < 3 hours	High Medium Low
Weather Events: Hurricane, Tornado, Crosswind	4. Highly Likely 3. Likely 2. Possible 1. Likely	4. Catastrophic 3. Critical 2. Limited 1. Negligible	4. Minimal 3. 6–1 hour 2. 12–24 hours 1. < 24 hours	4. 12+ hours 3. 6–12 hours 2. 3–6 hours 1. < 3 hours	High Medium Low
Bomb Threat/ Suspicious Items	4. Highly Likely 3. Likely 2. Possible 1. Likely	4. Catastrophic 3. Critical 2. Limited 1. Negligible	4. Minimal 3. 6–1 hour 2. 12–24 hours 1. < 24 hours	4. 12+ hours 3. 6–12 hours 2. 3–6 hours 1. < 3 hours	High Medium Low
Public Health Emergency: Epidemic Pandemic	4. Highly Likely 3. Likely 2. Possible 1. Likely	4. Catastrophic 3. Critical 2. Limited 1. Negligible	4. Minimal 3. 6–1 hour 2. 12–24 hours 1. < 24 hours	4. 12+ hours 3. 6–12 hours 2. 3–6 hours 1. < 3 hours	High Medium Low
Fire Safety	4. Highly Likely 3. Likely 2. Possible 1. Likely	4. Catastrophic 3. Critical 2. Limited 1. Negligible	4. Minimal 3. 6–1 hour 2. 12–24 hours 1. < 24 hours	4. 12+ hours 3. 6–12 hours 2. 3–6 hours 1. < 3 hours	High Medium Low

House of Worship Training (Title)

SIGN IN SHEET:

PRINT NAME	Miscellaneous changes: Address or email

Training Evaluation Form

Date of presentation:
Topic or Session:

Please complete the evaluation for today's training or exercise (drill); your feedback will be tallied and included in the After-Action Report or used for future training drills.

Criteria	Strongly Agree 4	Agree 3	Disagree 2
Training was relevant to my needs			
Materials provided were helpful			
Length of training (drill) was sufficient			
Content was well organized			
Questions were encouraged			
Instructions were clear and understandable			
Overall presentation met my expectations			
The presenter or presentation was effective			

Optional:
Name:
Title:

Organization or House of Worship

NAME OF HOUSE OF WORSHIP

<u>After-Action Report</u>

To: _____

From: _____

CC:_____

Date: _____/ Time: _____/ Location of Meeting:
_____

Purpose of Meeting: _____
_____

Meeting Objective: _____
_____
_____
_____

Summary Conclusions/Next Steps or Meeting/Location:
_____
_____

Prescripted: Response for Media Inquiry

If the media is at your church, you need time to assemble the facts for the initial press release statement. Getting and organizing the facts is a priority and it is important that your house of worship not give in to pressure to confirm or release information before you have confirmation from your clergy, emergency management partners, etc. The following responses may give you the necessary time to collect the facts. Use this "Template for your Press Statement" and for providing an initial press release statement after the facts are gathered.

Be sure you are authorized to give out the following information.
Date: _____ Time: _____
Approved by: _____

Prescripted responses:

If on the phone to media:

- Our worship house just learned about the situation and are trying to get more complete information at the moment.
- I am not the authority on this subject. Let me have (name) call you right back.
- How can I reach you when I have more information?
- All our efforts are directed at bringing the situation under control, so I am not going to speculate about the cause of the incident. How can I reach you when I have more information?
- We are preparing a statement on that now. Can I fax it to you in about (number) hours?
- You may check our website for background information, and I will (fax/email) you the time of the next update.

If in person at incident site or in front of press meeting:

This is an evolving emergency and I know you want as much information as possible—and so do we. I want to tell you what we can confirm right now.

At approximately (time), a (brief description of what happened).

At this point, we do not know the number of (persons ill, persons injured, injuries, deaths, etc.).

We have a (system, plan, procedure, operation) in place for just such an emergency, and we are being assisted by police, fire department, Federal Bureau of Investigation (FBI), Emergency Operation Center (EOC), and the Centers for Disease Control (CDC) as part of that plan.

The situation is (under) (not yet under) control and we are working with (local, state, federal) authorities to (contain this situation, determine how this happened, determine what actions may be needed by individuals, and the community to prevent this from happening again).

We will continue to gather information and release it to you as soon as possible. I will be back to you within (amount of time, two hours or less) to give you an update. As soon as we have more confirmed information, it will be provided. We ask for your patience as we respond to this emergency.

How to Write a Press Release

Guidance:

1. Formatting:
   The total length should be two pages, a minimum of four hundred to five hundred words preference
   Avoid using "I," "we," or "you."

   Font and format:
   Times New Roman or Calibri
   Bolded, larger heading
   Body of text should be single spaced
   One line of space between each paragraph

2. Church logo:
   Type church logo at the top center of the page.

3. Emailed press release:
   Use high resolution copy of the logo as a separate file.

4. Put the most important information first (just get to the facts):
   Reporters and editors are busy, so your press release must get their attention in the first paragraph. Give your primary news in the first paragraph.

5. Always use active voice:
   Use strong active language, get to the point.

6. Proofread the copy:
   Seek proofreading assistance when needed.

Church Logo and Press Release
FOR IMMEDIATE RELEASE
Email Address, Website URL
[Date]
[Headline]
[City], [State].

Begin your press release with a two-sentence paragraph that provides a quick overview of the news and why it is important. It should read easily and capture the reader's attention.

Next, provide relevant background information in understandable terms.

Depending upon the purpose of the press release, the final paragraph can be a brief description of your worship house. This should include a brief history of your worship house and clergy and types of services you offer if applicable.

SAMPLE:
Church Logo
October 26, 2019—Arson Attack at Calvary Baptist Church
CHICAGO, IL. The Calvary Baptist Church was attacked by an arsonist Saturday night. A flammable gasoline bomb was tossed near the entrance of the church, igniting shrubbery and trees. The church was not harmed. (State the local fire department.) At 10:00 p.m., a neighbor living in the vicinity saw an unidentified person running south on Allentown Road.

This disgusting attack is not representative of who we are, and we must find the persons responsible.

This church has been a staple in this community for one hundred years. A hate crime has never been committed, stated Rev. John Alexander, church clergy.

Congregation Members with Special Needs Survey

Member Information (Please Print)

First and Last Name: _____

Address, city, state, zip code: _____

_____

Phone: cell _____ home _____

	Yes	No	N/A
Do you live alone?			
If you live alone and are homebound, is there someone who checks on you regularly?			
Do you have a chronic or any medical condition?			
Do you need help getting around?			
Can you cook for yourself?			
Do you have an emergency plan?			
Do you have enough food, water, prescription medication, and supplies at home to last several days in case of emergency?			
Do you have a support animal?			
Do you have any other special needs? Please explain.			

Emergency Contact Information:

First and Last Name: _____

Address, city, state, zip code: _____

_____

Phone: cell _____ home _____

INJURY OR INCIDENT REPORT

This form should be completed after each injury or other emergency procedure. Accurate records should be maintained in a secure location. It is important to store the forms in case of insurance liability.

Date: _____

Injured Person: _____ Age: _____

Contact Information: _____

Completed by: _____Title: _____

Where were you when injury occurred: _____

Description of injury and how it occurred (add pages if additional space is needed):

_____

_____

_____

_____

_____

_____

Witnesses:

_____

_____

_____

_____

_____

Action taken (provide detailed description of medical action, CPR, etc.)

_____

_____

_____

_____

_____

(US) Occupational, Safety, and Health Administration

OSHA Inspection Questionnaire for Employees

Question	Completed	Needs Attention	Satisfactory	Not Needed
a) Do you keep training records for each employee on what safety topics they are trained in?				
b) Do you provide updated training revisions annually?				
c) Have you examined your administrative teams' workstations for ergonomic design?				
d) Do you provide maintenance or contractors with safety equipment (i.e., eyewear, earplugs, face masks, and hand protective equipment)? Do they exhibit proper use of all equipment consistently?				
e) Are your working areas safely maintained?				

f)	Do the maintenance staff bypass any safety guards or latches on lawn mowers or power equipment?				
g)	Is your cleaning staff trained on chemical storage and exposure risks?				
h)	Are your cleaning supplies labeled properly?				
i)	Do you have material safety data sheets for every chemical on-site?				
j)	Does your day care or childcare staff use latex gloves when dealing with blood or bodily fluids?				
k)	Does your staff know where to find fire extinguishers and defibrillator equipment?				
l)	Have your administrative staff been trained on how to use fire extinguishers and defibrillator equipment?				

Inspection Checklist Questions	Completed	Needs Attention	Satisfactory	Not Needed
13) If a medical center is not near your worship house, does at least one staff member have first aid certification?				
SECURITY PROTOCOL:				
1) Are your buildings kept locked when unoccupied?				
2) Is your building protected by a burglar alarm?				
3) Are keys to the building marked "Do not Copy"?				
4) Are the keys or access cards given out in limited numbers?				
5) Are locks and safe combinations changed when employees who have had access are discharged?				
6) Are personnel assigned to check windows and exit doors for security before leaving the building at the end of the day?				

7) Are all windows protected with window locks, wire mesh, or bars?				
8) Are all windows kept free of shrubbery and other obstructions behind which burglars can hide?				
9) Is a detailed written, photographic, or video inventory of building contents and valuables maintained? (The inventory should include brand, model number, serial number, cost, and date of purchase; receipts should be kept for new purchases.)				
10) Are sacred objects, vessels, and other valuables kept in a safe, vault, or quality locked cabinet when not in use?				
11) Is audio-visual, office, and musical equipment stored in a lock room or office area when not in use?				

12) Have you arranged for regular police patrols or a security force drive-by at night?				
13) Is sensitive student, employee, and volunteer information password protected and stored on a separate computer that does not have internet access?				
EMERGENCY PREPAREDNESS PROTOCOL:				
1) Has the house of worship written an emergency and safety plan?				
2) Have you completed a risk assessment in your current environment? Where are you vulnerable?				
3) Are congregants and volunteers trained at least annually in fire safety, evacuation, and disaster drills?				

4)	Has the worship house been inspected or received a security site assessment by law enforcement or crime prevention specialist to assess how safe it will be in the event of any disaster or security breech?				
5)	Have you selected a safety or security director? Who is in charge by title?				
6)	Are policies and procedures written to address active shooters and other violence?				
7)	When has your safety security plan been reviewed? Date:_____				
8)	Do you have a security committee?				
9)	Do you have designated safe rooms or shelter areas?				
10)	Has medical emergency training been provided (CPR, emergency defibrillator, and first aid training)?				

11) Do you have a health and safety committee and does it include a lead safety coordinator?				
12) Is basic medical emergency security and first aid training written in your plan?				
13) Do you have a mission statement?				
14) Do you have a trained, qualified medical lead? Name:_____				
15) Are emergency evacuation diagrams developed and posted throughout the building, identifying all exits, evacuation routes, safe assembly spaces, fire extinguishers, defibrillators, and first aid kits?				
16) Has the house of worship compiled a list of phone numbers, accounts, computer passwords, backup files, and addresses in a secure on- and off-campus area?				

17) Have arrangements been made ahead of time for an alternative meeting place, temporary worship space, and use of equipment?				
In Case of Fire:				
1) Are medical and fire emergencies practiced on a scheduled basis?				
2) Is the sprinkler system inspected annually?				
3) Are items stored within eighteen inches of any sprinkler heads?				
4) Are sprinkler heads that are exposed to potential physical damage protected with a metal guard?				
5) Are any items being hung from sprinkler heads? For example, holiday decorations?				
6) Is the area around the sprinkler system shut-off valve clear of all obstacles?				

7) Are the fire protection sensors unobstructed, operational, and periodically tested according to manufacture specifications by a certified contractor?				
8) Is the fire alarm system tested on an annual basis by a certified contractor?				
9) Are fire extinguishers and defibrillator equipment serviced according to local fire department and manufacturer specifications?				
10) Are flammable and combustible liquids appropriately marked and kept in a UL listed and locked flammable storage cabinet?				
11) Are candles only used under appropriate supervision?				
Heating, Ventilation, and Air Conditioning:				
1) Have all heating and cooling units been inspected?				

2) Are combustible materials kept at least thirty-six inches from the furnace or boiler?				
3) Are the boilers' inspection certificates posted in a boiler room?				
4) Is trash stored in enclosed containers placed outside daily or after use?				
5) Are cleaning products well marked and stored in a safe, locked place?				
6) Are all combustible materials (boxes, paper products, etc.) stored in appropriate locations and kept at least thirty-six inches away from any heating equipment or electrical panels?				
7) Are cleaning rags appropriately stored in metal containers with self-closing lids?				
8) Are buildings sump pumps and their battery backup tested?				

The Kitchen:				
1) Is the hood and ventilation system installed over the cooking equipment cleaned on a regular and periodic basis, including filters, hood, and duck work?				
2) Is the general cooking area clean and in good to excellent condition?				
3) Are proper food preparation protocols in place and being followed, including food preparation and serving, proper storage, and sanitation?				
4) Do you have a manual activation of the automatic fire suppression system? Have the kitchen staff employees trained to manually activate the system when needed?				

5) Is the automatic fire suppression system protecting the deep fat fryers and grease producing appliances? Are they serviced by a certified contractor according to appliance specifications? Are your fire extinguishers available when needed?			
Legal Liability, Insurance, and Security:			
1) Do you have an accident prevention policy or mission statement?			
2) Are there written performance and accountability standards and objectives for house of worship managers and leadership?			
3) Do you have emergency response procedures including notification of authorities, parents, next of kin, and church officials?			

4) Are emergency phone numbers posted by all telephones and cell phone contact lists? Are they available in off-site locations?				
5) Do you have a written standard of conduct for adults and children including other relationships, establishing parameters of conduct, and contact during and after normal activity hours?				
6) Does the written standard include parameters for online conduct and contact with children and youth, including e-mail and social networking sites?				
7) Are parents fully informed about the activities their children will be involved in?				

8) Do ushers, servers, volunteers, and leadership have guidelines to follow when dealing with the indigent, homeless for mentally ill visitors and congregants?				
9) Is there offering protocol procedures? Are offerings properly transported by security and designees and recorded by a team of two or more nonrelated individuals.				
10) Are offerings immediately deposited in a bank or night depository? Are checks stamped "For Deposit Only" immediately upon receipt?				
11) When the house of worship is used by outside groups, is there a person designated to record who attends meetings, gatherings, weddings to ensure your campus is always secure?				

12) Have local laws been researched to determine requirements for hiring security guards?				
13) Are security guards properly vetted, screened, trained, and supervised? Do they hold proper up-to-date license permits?				
14) If hired security services are used, have consultations with an attorney, local law enforcement, and insurance agent been done to determine the feasibility of using such services?				
15) Are armed guards properly licensed, hold necessary permits, and only carry legal and authorized weapons?				
16) Have ushers, greeters, and leaders been trained on how to handle violent situations or house of worship violence?				

Business Impact Analysis (BIA) and Continuity of Operations (COOP) for Houses of Worship

NOTE: TWO SIGNATURES AND TWO KEYS ARE REQUIRED TO ACCESS ALL EMERGENCY

DOCUMENTS.

Plan to Stay in Current Worship House:

_____ Name:
_____ Address:
_____ City, State, Country:
_____ Telephone Number:
_____ Cell Number:
_____ Email Address:

If this location in not accessible. We will operate from the alternate location below:

_____ Name:
_____ Address:
_____ City, State, Country:
_____ Telephone Number:
_____ Cell Number:
_____ Email Address:

The following person is our primary contact and will serve as the congregation's spokesperson in an emergency.

_____ Name:
_____ Address:
_____ City, State, Country:

_____ Telephone Number:
_____ Cell Number:
_____ Email Address:

If the person is unavailable, the alternate person will succeed in managing this crisis.

_____ Name and Title of
_____ Primary Contact:
_____ Address:
_____ City, State, Country:
_____ Telephone Number:
_____ Cell Number:
_____ Email Address:

Contractors and Vendors:

Company Name:

_____ Address:
City, State, Zip
_____ Code, Country:
Phone: _____ Fax:_____
_____ Email Address:
_____ Contact Names:

Materials or Services Provided:

_____
_____
_____
_____
_____

Alternate Vendors (we will obtain supplies and materials from):

_____

_____

_____

_____

_____

Communication Protocol:

Protocol for communication with our congregants, volunteers, and others:

_____

_____

_____

_____

_____

Protocol for communication with our staff:

_____

_____

_____

_____

_____

Cyber Security Protocol:

To protect our computer hardware, we will:

_____

_____

_____

_____

To protect our computer software, we will:

_____

_____

_____

_____

_____

If our computers are destroyed, we will use our back-up computers at the following location:

_____

_____

_____

_____

_____

Record Backup Protocol:

Name and title of persons: _____,
is responsible for backing up our critical records including payroll and accounting systems.

Backup records including a copy of the emergency plan documents, site maps, insurance policies, bank account records, and computer backup documents are stored on-site:

_____

_____

_____

_____

_____

Another set of backup records are stored at the following off-site location:

_____

_____

_____

_____

_____

If our accounting and payroll records are destroyed, we will provide for continuity using the following protocol/methods:

_____

_____

_____

_____

_____

NOTE: TWO SIGNATURES AND TWO KEYS ARE REQUIRED TO ACCESS ALL EMERGENCY DOCUMENTS.

_____

_____

_____

_____

_____

Risk Assessment Worksheet (Identified Threats and Hazards and Risk Assessment)

The risk assessment test is recommended for updates annually.

Hazard	Probability	Magnitude	Warning	Duration	Risk Priority
Active Shooter Event	4. Highly Likely 3. Likely 2. Possible 1. Likely	4. Catastrophic 3. Critical 2. Limited 1. Negligible	4. Minimal 3. 6–1 hour 2. 12–24 hours 1. < 24 hours	4.12+ hours 3. 6–12 hours 2. 3–6 hours 1. < 3 hours	High Medium Low
Hostage Situation	4. Highly Likely 3. Likely 2. Possible 1. Likely	4. Catastrophic 3. Critical 2. Limited 1. Negligible	4. Minimal 3. 6–1 hour 2. 12–24 hours 1. < 24 hours	4.12+ hours 3. 6–12 hours 2. 3–6 hours 1. < 3 hours	High Medium Low
Weather Events: Hurricane, Tornado, Crosswind	4. Highly Likely 3. Likely 2. Possible 1. Likely	4. Catastrophic 3. Critical 2. Limited 1. Negligible	4. Minimal 3. 6–1 hour 2. 12–24 hours 1. < 24 hours	4. 12+ hours 3. 6–12 hours 2. 3–6 hours 1. < 3 hours	High Medium Low
Bomb Threat/ Suspicious Items	4. Highly Likely 3. Likely 2. Possible 1. Likely	4. Catastrophic 3. Critical 2. Limited 1. Negligible	4. Minimal 3. 6–1 hour 2. 12–24 hours 1. < 24 hours	4. 12+ hours 3. 6–12 hours 2. 3–6 hours 1. < 3 hours	High Medium Low
Medical Emergency: Public Health Emergencies (Epidemic, Pandemic)	4. Highly Likely 3. Likely 2. Possible 1. Likely	4. Catastrophic 3. Critical 2. Limited 1. Negligible	4. Minimal 3. 6–1 hour 2. 12–24 hours 1. < 24 hours	4. 12+ hours 3. 6–12 hours 2. 3–6 hours 1. < 3 hours	High Medium Low
Fire Safety	4. Highly Likely 3. Likely 2. Possible 1. Likely	4. Catastrophic 3. Critical 2. Limited 1. Negligible	4. Minimal 3. 6–1 hour 2. 12–24 hours 1. < 24 hours	4. 12+ hours 3. 6–12 hours 2. 3–6 hours 1. < 3 hours	High Medium Low

REFERENCES

This plan has been developed in accordance with guidance provided in the following publications, references, and sources:

- Are You Ready Guide to Citizen Preparedness Federal Emergency Management Agency (FEMA)
- Business Continuity and Disaster Preparedness Plan, www. freechurchforms.com
- CDC Centers for Disease Control and Prevention, Coronavirus Disease 2019 (COVID-19)
- CDC emergency preparedness and response site, http:// emergency.cdc.gov/planning/
- Church Mutual Insurance Company, Risk Control Central, Merrill, WI (Self-Inspection Checklist)
- CISF International, Critical Incident Stress Foundation, Understanding CISM
- Council on American Islamic Relations (CAIR) Hate Graffiti on New York Mosque
- Democracynow.org (Tree of Life Synagogue Article)
- Emergency Management Safety and Security Plan, Mount Calvary AME Church, 2019
- Faith-based and Community Organizations Pandemic Influenza Checklist. US Centers for Disease Control and Prevention (2006) FEMA: "Developing Emergency Operations Plans for Houses of Worship" Guide, June 2013
- FEMA: Federal Emergency Management Agency, National Continuity Program,

FEMA-NCP-Federal-Continuity@dhs.gov, Prepare Your Business for an Emergency
- Fire Safety Plan (Universal) National Fire Protection Association (Codes & Standards) NFPA 4
- Homeland Security, House of Worship Security Practices Guide, May 2013
- INSURANCE JOURNAL, May 22, 2020, https//www.insurance Journal.com/news/international
- Jean Marie Stine, *Writing Successful Self-Help & How to Books* (Wiley & Sons, Inc., 1997)
- Maryland Emergency Operations Plan Guidance
- Maryland Hurricane Preparedness Guide
- Maryland Natural Hazards Preparedness Guide
- Maryland Natural Hazards Preparedness Guide Constellation Energy and
  Maryland Emergency Management Agency (MEMA)
- Michael Bremer, *Untechnical Writing* (Untechnical Pr, 1999)
- National Disaster Interfaith Network, New York, Continuity of Operations Planning (COOP)
- National Institute of Justice Protocols (NIJ)
- National Institute of Mental Health, Post Traumatic Health Disorders (PTSD)
- New/New Zealand, alijazeerce.com
- Preparation and Planning for Public Health Emergencies (website)
- Psychology Today.com, What is a Critical Incident?
- Robert A. Caro, *Working: Researching, Interviewing, Writing* (Bodley Head, 2019)
- The Baltimore County Office of Homeland Security
- The Occupational Safety and Health Administration (OSHA) Guidance for Houses of Worship (website)
- The US Department of Homeland Security Notice of Funding Opportunity (NOFO)FY 2018 Nonprofit

Security Grant Program (NSGP) credit Maryland Emergency Management Agency (MEMA)

- Todd C. Frankel, "Insurers knew the Damage a Viral Pandemic Could Wreak on Businesses. So, they excluded coverage," *Washington Post*, April 2, 2020.
- US Center for Disease Control and Prevention (n.d.)
- US Department of Health and Human Services: US Centers for Disease Control and Prevention: http://www. flu.gov//planning   preparedness/community/faith-based community checklist
- United States Department of Labor (OSHA)
- United States federal laws governing defendants with mental diseases and defects
  [18.S.C. 4241-4248]
- World Health Organization, who.int

INDEX

ABOUT THE AUTHOR

Lauren Holley-Allen is a retired psychiatrist assistant with Glass Health Systems and a retired training administrator with the Maryland Emergency Management Agency (MEMA) in Reisterstown, Maryland, and the Maryland Department of the Military. Her responsibilities included training management for state, local, private, and volunteer emergency management disciplines. Lauren managed various activities of the Emergency Preparedness Training Program for MEMA's employees and community first responders, representatives, and agencies.

Lauren previously served as the state training officer for MEMA and the director of education and training for the Department of Health and Mental Hygiene (DHMH) at Clifton T. Perkins Hospital and the Developmental Disabilities Administration as training director, coordinator, and mental health consultant.

Mrs. Holley-Allen's career spans over thirty years of state service, in which she first joined DHMH and DDA as a master's-level psychologist in 1985.

Additionally, she worked as a consultant for Glass Health Systems and Union Memorial Hospital. She developed and taught diversity training for psychiatric interns who worked in emergency rooms with physically and emotionally challenged minority patients. She provided psychiatric consultation and training for area hospitals, nursing homes, and special education students and faculty in local schools. She coauthored a publication titled "Counseling the Chronically Health Impaired Student," as part of her graduate thesis.

Mrs. Holley-Allen received her undergraduate degree from Morgan State University in mental health and hospital administration and her master's degree from Antioch University in behavioral and counseling psychology. On September 26, 2018, she was presented with the Albert Nelson Marquis Lifetime Achievement Award as a leader in the mental health profession.

She is one of ten psychiatric/physician's assistants licensed in the state of Maryland and was responsible for the Physicians Continuing Medical Education Program accredited with the Maryland State Medical Society (Med/Chi) at the Clifton T. Perkins Psychiatric Forensic Hospital. She was responsible for both employees' and patients' safety and emergency preparedness training.

Mrs. Holley-Allen actively participates in her community at the Mount Calvary AME Church, Community Development Corporation (CDC) board member, Beads of Wisdom Bible Study, Baltimore Heritage Quilters Guild, and Maryland Miniature Enthusiast of Baltimore County.

Mrs. Holley-Allen's perspective is "Lifetime learning and preparedness makes the difference." She proclaims, "I am a public servant who strives to meet the challenges of continued excellence."

CPSIA information can be obtained
at www.ICGtesting.com
Printed in the USA
BVHW091242270921
617614BV00027B/889